GET PAID WHAT YOU'RE WORTH

Using **Tax Planning** to Get **Paid** For Your **Expertise**

By **DOMINIQUE MOLINA**, CPA, CTC

Copyright © 2016 Certified Tax Coach™, LLC

All rights reserved. No part of this book may be used or reproduced in any manner whatsoever without prior written consent of the authors, except as provided by the United States of America copyright law.

Published by Certified Tax Coach™, LLC, Las Vegas, NV

Certified Tax Coach™ is a registered trademark

Printed in the United States of America.

ISBN: 978-0-9832341-7-3

This publication is designed to provide accurate and authoritative information with regard to the subject matter covered. It is sold with the understanding that the publisher is not engaged in rendering legal, accounting, or other professional advice. If legal advice or other expert assistance is required, the services of a competent professional should be sought. The opinions expressed by the authors in this book are not endorsed by Certified Tax Coach™ and are the sole responsibility of the author rendering the opinion.

This title is available at special quantity discounts for bulk purchases for sales promotions, premiums, fundraising, and educational use. Special versions or book excerpts can also be created to fit specific needs.

For more information, please write:

Certified Tax Coach, LLC™, 8885 Rio San Diego Drive Ste 237 San Diego, CA 92108

or call 1.888.582.9752

Visit us online at www.CertifiedTaxCoach.com

TABLE OF CONTENTS

FOREWORD
By Ronald J. Baker, the father of value pricing for accountants
"You will never get paid more than you think you're worth.
It's past time for our profession to capture the value our customers already know we provide."

vii

CHAPTER 1
Have You Built a Business or a Job?
"Owning a business as an employee traps you into an endless cycle of work and your income depends on your ability to produce."

1

CHAPTER 2
Get Paid for Your Expertise: Value-Pricing Your Services
"The key to getting paid what you're worth without doing thousands of tax returns is to change your clients' viewpoint that there is a going rate and that they can pay any accountant to do the job."

19

CHAPTER 3
Value Pricing: Good for Your Clients—and You
"One of the best benefits of value pricing is that you can show people how to get your service for free! (Even if the price is 10 times higher than you've ever charged.)"

37

CHAPTER 4
How to Use Leverage and Scale a Tax Business

"Your ability to scale your tax business depends on your ability to charge premium fees that are not attached to the amount of time your work takes you to complete."

45

CHAPTER 5
Value-Pricing Your Services

"Many professionals subconsciously fear the use of value pricing. On some level, the ambiguity of the value of services traditionally offered by accountants creates confusion over how consumers view and value their work."

55

CHAPTER 6
Selling Premium-Fee Tax Plans

"When you offer tax planning to your clients and focus on the value and savings you can create for them, they want this service; you are practically offering them money, and they will be willing to pay more for such a service."

69

CHAPTER 7
Using a Tax Rescue to Sell Planning Services

"How can you effectively use a tax return to sell planning services? There is a secret formula for this that will leave people eager to hire you at premium fees to 'rescue' them."

79

CHAPTER 8

Cherry-Picking Clients and Identifying Opportunities

"Imagine being in a position to handpick your clients, to work only with people you actually enjoy, to work with those who happily pay your fees—on time."

91

CHAPTER 9

Maintaining the Health of Your Tax Business

"Creating a business health process for you and your clients will add more value to your relationship and provide additional services to offer and include in your monthly fixed-price agreements."

101

CHAPTER 10

Maintaining the Health of Your Tax Business— Getting (and Keeping) Clients

"If you're looking to improve the type of clients you work with, and find quality, premium-fee clients, it may require some marketing."

117

CHAPTER 11

Getting It All Done—How to Create the 25-Hour Day to Implement Your Changes

"If you want to drastically change the way you are pricing your services, you're going to need to make the time to do this important work."

125

CONCLUSION

"Learn the three easy steps to increasing your job satisfaction, giving you the freedom you deserve, and getting paid what you're worth."

133

Foreword

Ronald J. Baker

Someone once asked the physicist Albert Michelson why he worked so hard on measuring the speed of light; he replied he did it because it was such great fun.

Ever since I made it publicly known that my purpose in life was to bury the billable hour and timesheets across all professional firms, I have frequently been asked how I came to seek this rather strange quest.

One answer is because, like Michelson, it is great fun to challenge the conventional wisdom of your colleagues and try to persuade them there is a better way.

Another answer is that I have met some astounding people along the way who share my passion for improving the professions for posterity. One of those people is Dominique Molina. Her crusade to better the tax profession is infectious.

In *Get Paid What You're Worth*, you'll learn many valuable lessons:

- How to work ON your business rather than just IN your business, building a sustainable business model that creates real value for your customers and yourself;
- Why industry-standard pricing and the idea that tax services are a commodity are deadly illusions;
- That time spent ("billable hours") has nothing to do with value to the customer. Time is not a resource; it's a constraint that makes you prioritize your activities;

- Tax planning should be mandatory for all CPA customers. If they don't need tax planning, they probably don't need a CPA. We don't want surgeons piercing ears;
- How to get rid of low-value work with the 4-D strategies (Delete it, Delegate it, Defer it, or Design it out);
- The many deleterious effects of hourly billing and why you should provide price certainty to your customers (one reason: because it can command a price premium, just as fixed-rate mortgages do over variable-rate mortgages);
- Why value pricing is far more advantageous than hourly billing, and makes for higher customer satisfaction, loyalty, and profitability for the firm;
- How to replicate your best customers and avoid Baker's Law: Bad Customers Drive Out Good Customers.

The above lessons, and more, are illustrated with stories from Dominique, and other practitioners who have implemented these strategies. Study success, as it often leaves clues.

After I read *Get Paid What You're Worth*, I was reminded of a story that I think is worth passing on.

When Larry Page and Sergey Brin were students at Stanford, they developed technology that was designed to search Stanford University's Web pages, which immediately became popular among the students and faculty. This was 1996, and everyone thought that Yahoo! was the dominant search engine, and there could never be another one. Larry and Sergey did not think their technological innovation was the basis for the company they wanted to start, so they put it on the market—at a price of approximately $1 million.

Fortunately for the rest of us, there were no takers. Had they found a buyer, Google probably never would have been born. It is an excellent example of how overpricing can have salutary effects.

In today's world, human capital is the source of 80% of the developed world's wealth. After all, the Neanderthal in his cave had all the resources at his disposal as we have today. The difference between his standard of living and ours is the amount of knowledge they could apply to those resources to provide goods and services of value.

Napoleon Hill wrote in *Think and Grow Rich*: "There is no standard price on ideas. The creator of ideas makes his own price, and, if he is smart, gets it."

In other words, you will never get paid more than you think you're worth.

It's past time for our profession to capture the value our customers already know we provide.

Dominique's book will greatly assist you in that objective, thereby keeping our profession relevant, adaptable, and capable of creating value far into the future.

Ronald J. Baker
Radio host on the VoiceAmerica show: *The Soul of Enterprise: Business in the Knowledge Economy*, founder of VeraSage Institute, LinkedIn Influencer, and author of *The Firm of the Future*; *Mind Over Matter*; *Measure What Matters to Customers*; and *Implementing Value Pricing: A Radical Business Model for Professional Firms*.
www.thesoulofenterprise.com
www.verasage.com
@ronaldbaker

Complimentary Pricing Essentials Tool Kit

Includes:

Worksheets from this book

Price Increase Announcement Template

Price Increase Package Opt-In Certificate Template

Price Offer Opt-Out Certificate Template

Audit Protection Package Profit Analyzer

Get Paid What You're Worth Home Video Course

Just visit www.GetPaidForYourWorth.com

CHAPTER 1

Have you Built a Business or a Job?

How many hours a week, on average, do you work for your business? If you're like most tax professionals, you're working 50-70 hours per week year round, and even more during peak seasons. This doesn't count time you spend at home checking and responding to emails, calls you receive and make while away from the office, and even your "rest time" you spend thinking about your business: the deadlines, IRS notices, "quick questions" from clients, and other worries that occupy your mind.

Do you still enjoy the business you are building, or has it somehow turned into more of a job—with you being your own worst boss? Many tax pros start a business because they think they can run it how they want, take as much time off as they want, and keep all the profits. Perhaps you had something specific in mind when you started: weekends off, holidays with family, time on the golf course? But ask yourself, when was the last time you took more than one week off, completely free of work? How many weeks of vacation have you averaged in the last five years? And when you were last away from the office, how was it when you returned? Was it operating smoothly, bringing in the same billings, meeting key deadlines, and cultivating new prospects? Or did you find a mess, declined billings, and unproductive employees enjoying their time while the boss was away?

The irony is that while most tax professionals start a tax business to provide freedom for themselves and their families, most find that they have actually created a prison.

Instead of control, they experience chaos, and instead of autonomy, most are restricted to their desks in an effort to survive the workload and keep enough cash coming in to meet their obligations. In a sense, they have created the worst kind of job there is: one with much more responsibility than employees with set schedules have, and without any of the perks they hoped to enjoy as business owners.

One of the biggest problems today for accountants is that they are working themselves to the bone because they can't charge enough in tax preparation fees to earn the freedom that owning a business is supposed to bring them. This especially is true for small business accountants. By underestimating your worth, you're losing the dream of running a lucrative tax practice.

In order to correct or even avoid this problem altogether, you must change your ways of doing business SALY (same as last year). You must promote yourself from worker bee to real-life business owner. Yet, it takes more than a change in your job description to experience the freedom that owning a business is supposed to bring. I propose that it is only when you build a true enterprise, one that is independent of any one person and can grow and develop in a healthy way, that you will free yourself from the bondage created by old and tired methods of running a tax practice.

This chapter is not only going to help you identify "old business" strategies, including old pricing models, it will also demonstrate how to conduct "new business," which is the business that will ensure you get paid what you're worth.

Assessing Your Current Business Approach

To start, ask yourself, "Am I stuck?" I want you to look at where you are currently and critically assess where you're stuck in your business. Consider the following questions:

- Is this how you dreamed your business would be?
- Is your business growing every year? At what rate? Are you satisfied with that level of growth?
- Will the current growth rate of your business provide for your future cash needs and exit strategy?
- Has your business decreased because of the recession or other factors?
- Has your life changed, and does your business reflect those changes in the way that you would like?
- Are there things that you want to do with your business that you haven't had the chance to do yet?
- Do you want more challenges?
- If you evaluated the time you spend on enjoyable things at work, would you be satisfied with the result?

These questions are important in becoming self-aware of the current status of your business. Your dream of owning a tax practice may have gone down a different path than you originally intended. Because of various circumstances, you may not be reaping the rewards you desire. You may even feel stuck because you're ready to move forward in your business and you might not be sure quite how to do that.

Dominique's Story

I started my first "real" business at age 22 when I was completing my junior year in college. I was struggling to pay my way through school with a part-time job while I attended full-time classes for my accounting degree. Since I had been balancing my parents' checkbook since the age of eight, independent bookkeeping provided a natural way to earn a higher hourly wage, so I could afford to maintain shorter hours and devote more time to my studies. I jumped into business out of necessity to earn more income. I didn't really treat it as a real business, and I didn't have a business plan or a marketing strategy, but that didn't stop me from creating an income. As for a business name? That didn't come until my first tax return, and I quickly adopted the name of my baby brother's imaginary friend.

Lesson Learned: I discovered that I could earn more income by connecting my compensation to my expertise rather than to physical efforts.

Why Did You Start a Tax Practice?

The initial step in assessing your current business approach is remembering why you started a tax practice in the first place. Obviously, accountants start their own tax business with certain goals in mind. However, once the ball gets rolling and the projects start to pile up, it can be easy to lose sight of those original goals.

Have you ever taken the time to think about why you started a tax practice in the first place? Perhaps you started your business because you're an independent person. Maybe you wanted more free time to do things you enjoy. You may have started your own tax practice because you believed there would be more financial opportunity than if you worked for someone else.

Dominique's Story

Early Practice Phase

After completing my degree in accounting, obtaining my CPA license, and completing my experience with the largest local CPA firm in San Diego, I decided to launch my own CPA firm. Together with a colleague from the larger firm, we set out to offer a full-service CPA practice with audit and tax services. Not having learned much from my first business experience, my second business also began without a business plan or marketing strategy. I just didn't see the need since my first business had been what I considered successful. Surprisingly, I didn't need traditional marketing. I launched my business at a time when websites were just beginning to be commonplace. By merely creating a page and posting it live, prospects found me and signed on for tax services.

As work came in, I responded, and soon we had a decent revenue stream. I didn't mind working nights and weekends as my business was growing. I figured I needed to take advantage of the opportunities, because who knew if I would have enough work next month, or next year. Soon, I needed more than just a Starbucks to meet with clients, so my partner and I rented a small office. Although I found myself not enjoying every client I worked with, again I figured I might not have enough work to provide the income I would need in the future or to cover my growing overhead. I saw each project as a business opportunity and readily accepted what was in front of me.

Lesson Learned: Despite operating without a marketing plan, there never seemed to be a shortage of work. And even though I feared running out at some point, I began to think after several years that perhaps I might have had sufficient work even without accepting everything that came my way.

Evaluating Your Success

Using the awareness of your current status is a large part of evaluating your current level of success, but you also need to assess your current achievements. Are you where you'd hoped you'd be at this stage in your development? Recognizing that success is a subjective experience based on one's expectations and actual outcomes, for evaluative purposes, most people believe earnings to be a global indicator of success. The fact that earnings are quantifiable allows us to be comparative both in our initial desires of beginning our entrepreneurship journey versus our current state as well as in our experiences as peers.

Given that accountants practice in various specialties, it is human nature to look for ways to make a comparable analysis despite nuances in our work. One such way to make earnings comparable despite the fact that we are being compensated for different work done is to revert to the age-old practice of examining hourly wage.

In the history of wage labor, earnings are typically exchanged for time spent at work. As classicist Moses I. Finley writes in *The Ancient Economy* (1973):

> "The very idea of wage-labour requires two difficult conceptual steps. First it requires the abstraction of a man's labour from both his person and the product of his work. When one purchases an object from an independent craftsman...one has not bought his labour but the object, which he has produced in his own time and under his own conditions of work. But when one hires labour, one purchases an abstraction, labour-power, which the purchaser then uses at a time and under conditions which he, the purchaser, not the 'owner' of the labour-power, determines (and for which he normally pays after he consumed it). Second, the wage labour system requires the establishment of a method of measuring the labour one has purchased, for purposes of payment, commonly by introducing a second abstraction, namely labour-time."

(Side note: The invention of the clock coincided with the use of time for work as a way to subdivide time spent on labor.)

As Finley puts it, when being compensated for labor, you don't consider the outcome or "product of labor," just the effort or input of the laborer. And so, as the saying goes, the sands of time run through the hourglass; despite centuries that have passed, most professionals (and consumers) still use the hourly wage as a quantitative element with which to compare earnings.

In keeping with this age-old method of evaluation, what are your current hourly earnings? It stands to reason that to gain clarity on the current state of your business, you must identify where you stand.

How Much Do You Really Earn?

When was the last time you determined your hourly earnings? You might find yourself not wanting to know—perhaps even avoiding the subject. Many tax business owners fool themselves into a denial that they earn their quoted hourly rate for client work. But do you really make that much?

When I first started my bookkeeping service at the age of 22, I could easily determine my actual earnings, and I was quite happy with the result. Twenty dollars per hour at that time was more money than I had ever made, and it met my needs. During this time, my brother and sister-in-law were completing medical school. They used to joke around during their residency days about how little they actually made per hour after factoring in all the hours they were working as compared to their income. Later on in my business evolution, when I owned a tax accounting business with a typical pricing model, I completed the exercise to show I was different than a medical resident. Despite working long hours that sounded similar to clinical rotations, I was confident that the results of this exercise would show that my high hourly billings netted me more profit.

Let's see if the same holds true for you. The goal of this activity is to calculate the hours you're dedicating to your business and the dollar amount of your profit to find out what you're really bringing home.

Complete the exercise using the formula below; you can even begin filling in the dollar amounts before I walk you through it:

Figure 1.1 How Much Do You Really Earn?

Quoted Hourly Rate:	$_____
Total Firm Profit:	$_____
Net Income:	$_____
+ Officer's Compensation and Benefits:	$_____
= Total Officer's Profit:	$_____
÷ Total Hours Worked:	#_____
= Real Hourly Rate:	$_____

First, in the space next to "Total Firm Profit," fill in your firm revenues and the hourly rate you quote for consulting work. These amounts are not included in this equation; I only ask you to list your firm's profit total to use as a reference point once you've calculated the Real Hourly Rate.

Next, fill in your "Net Income" on the third line. Make sure you reflect the net income dollar amount after deducting all of the bills and overhead you pay. If you don't have your exact numbers available, simply use estimates for this exercise. You don't have to be exact, although I'm sure you have a good idea of how much net income you're earning.

On the fourth line, enter the value of any officer's compensation or benefits that may have been included in overhead to add in the value of income you've effectively taken out of the business for your own needs. Note: if you merely take home profit distributions, then it is alright to leave "Officer's Compensation and Benefits" blank.

The fifth line represents "Total Officer's Profit," and to arrive at this amount, you just need to add line items three and four.

Next, you're going to enter the total number of hours worked on the sixth line. Honesty and accuracy is of great importance here. You need to consider all of the hours you labored during the entire year. The following are things to consider when determining this figure:

- All of the evening hours you worked
- All of the weekend hours you worked
- Holidays you spent working
- Lunch hours or mealtimes missed because of work
- Leisure, family, or vacation time spent distracted by work

Once you have determined the amount of hours you actually worked during the year, you can effectively answer the question, "How much do you really earn?" Refer back to the original equation and take the "Total Officer's Profit" from the fifth line of this activity and divide that by the total number of hours worked you indicated on the sixth line. As a result, you will arrive at your "True Hourly Wage" on the seventh and final line.

As an example, Figure 1.2 shows a completed "How Much Do You Really Earn?" equation.

Figure 1.2 How Much Do You Really Earn?

Quoted Hourly Rate:	$300
Total Firm Profit:	$317,000
Net Income:	$18,000
+ Officer's Compensation and Benefits:	$134,000
= Total Officer's Profit:	$152,000
÷ Total Hours Worked:	3,800
= Hourly Wage:	$40

Figure 1.2. represents the totals I wrote in when I first completed this exercise years ago. At the time, my hourly billing rate was $300 per hour, but this exercise revealed I was making less than $40 per hour—much to my disappointment. That was the reality that set forth my mission to get paid what I'm worth.

Dominique's Story

Early Business Phase

After several years of running the partnership with my friend and starting a family, I noticed I wasn't spending as much time as I wanted to at home with my son. Like most tax accountants, I thought the best way to make more money and have more free time was to hire others to do the work. Since my business depended on me to bring in revenue, I decided I needed to hire employees to work while I spent more time at home with my family. I figured that in order to hire employees, I needed to market my business and bring in new work. I set aside cash to begin some direct mail and coupon advertising campaigns and sought a larger office space. My longtime partner did not agree with my plans to grow the business and felt satisfied with the contract work he was receiving regularly as an auditor. We decided to split the partnership and amicably separated.

While I moved forward with the expansion plans, my anxiety grew over the growing marketing and overhead costs, but I didn't know any other way to reduce my time at work and balance my family life with my need to maintain my income level. Before long, my first staff was trained and ready for tax season.

Depending on what you wrote on line seven as your hourly wage, you may be either thrilled or wincing in pain. Now, remember that the only purpose of the first line is to show you how much money the firm is taking in as compared to how much you're actually making per hour you work. You might be completely satisfied with the amount of money you earn per hour compared to your firm's profit total. Conversely, you might be surprised when you're looking at how much you really earn based on your inputs of effort. At the peak of my tax business, I was working about 70 hours per week. I was burned out, maxed out, and exhausted. I intended to prove I made much more than my hourly rate, and even that I could reduce my hours at the office and still afford my lifestyle. I discovered that to reduce my hours to a "normal" 40-hour week, I would also reduce my income. When I saw the result, I noticed that working a normal work schedule would create an income level similar to my clients with cushy government jobs. Jobs with five weeks of annual vacation, off at five, no working at home, freedom. I was green with envy! The grass certainly seemed greener on the other side. Further, this exercise only reveals the dollars and cents behind your labor. There are a lot of non-monetary things that your business can cost you as well; these factors can really start to affect how you feel about your business.

Don't ignore the costs on your personal life. You may have given up significant opportunities as a result of your current practices. Some of these non-monetary costs include:

- Family time
- Hobbies
- Personal relationships
- Other business opportunities
- Health
- Other life goals and desires

While it is difficult to place a dollar value on these important subjects, you must evaluate the opportunity cost relative to your earnings. If you recognize that you have sacrificed areas of personal interest in favor of your business, you must include the foregone value of that choice in order to calculate your true earnings.

Now that you've calculated how much you're really earning, ask yourself: Is your true hourly rate higher than you expected? Is it lower than you expected? Is the figure that you came up with commensurate with your education and experience? Is this the business level you feel you should be operating on at this point of your career? Look at the value of the work you are providing—is it more than what you earn? Are you getting paid what you're worth?

What Type of Business Do You Operate?

Now that you've examined your real earnings, let's examine other costs of your tax business. Michael Gerber of E-Myth fame describes the accounting business as being one of three stages of business. First, your business can be a practice, and most firms actually start out this way. He uses the term "practice" to describe a business where the accountant is the business; the accountant basically acts as an employee or a technician in his or her own business and has essentially created a job for the purpose of being employed. I like to refer to this type of business as "employee-owned." Gerber describes the concept of having this type of business as the most limited form of business possible because it's built around the technician—in this case, the technician is the tax business owner. The negative aspects to having an employee-owned business are numerous. There's no one to fill in when you are sick or need to be away for other things in your life. If you want to take a vacation, the work will still be there when you return, and making money while you are away doesn't happen at this level of a tax practice. When you consider the typical role of an employee in a business, they are there to perform labor. Although the employees physically perform the work, the labor itself is owned by the business, according to Finley, and used as the business determines. This may help you understand why at times your business and schedule feel out of control. In reality, working in an employee-owned business, you aren't in control of your labor, the business is!

Gerber calls the second, more sophisticated business operation a "business." A business features other people besides the accountant as well as a system by which the business does what it does. Still, it's heavily dependent on the owner, and even though the owner has developed some control over the business, he or she really doesn't have any freedom from the business at this level. I refer to this style of business as "manager-owned." When working in a business with lower-level staff, by default you are the manager even if you don't consider yourself one. You may find staff and systems helpful in allowing you to step away for brief periods of time, but in a manager-owned business, it won't be long before the business stops producing as it is still dependent on you as manager to survive. As a manager, you are still really being compensated for your inputs, although your responsibilities are probably greater given the fact that you are responsible for other's labor inputs as well. Many tax business owners find themselves in this ownership style struggling to survive the workload one deadline to the next.

The last level of business, the "enterprise," Gerber claims can only be achieved once the accountant has finally mastered all the systems and processes, and every person working for the accountant possesses an important role. An enterprise is the kind of business that brings an income whether the owner is physically there or not. An enterprise is a business that can survive into perpetuity without the owner. This third and highest level of business offers total control and total freedom. For this reason, I refer to this style of business ownership as "investor-owned." Consider the responsibilities of an investor, for example. As an investor in Apple stock, I'm not required to be at the company to earn income. In evaluating my investment, I check the financial statements of the company, but the company's profit does not relate in any way to my inputs. If you desire a business that operates completely independently of you or anyone else, build an investor-owned business.

I've adapted Gerber's philosophy into my own thinking. I realized one reason a business can't provide freedom for the owner is because of how the business is owned. Owning a business as an employee traps you into an endless cycle of work, and your income depends on your ability to produce. Although you may hire additional staff to help relieve you of this pressure, owning your business as a manager still means the business relies on you to produce income and value. Only when you own your business as an investor will you fully experience the freedom of owning an independent business. These three ownership types—employee, manager, and investor—are the framework for building a business that provides income with or without you.

Dominique's Story

That first tax season with a new staff of five was challenging. I was disappointed that instead of reducing my hours at work, the new staff and the marketing efforts my growing business demanded required me to work even more than before! And although people were technically competent, I didn't have any clear processes and procedures to follow and again found myself in the position of missing income if I wasn't at work to earn it. Even worse than before though, I had now added a new burden to my workload—always having work for the staff to keep them busy, and always needing income to ensure that I could make my payroll. Just to get through tax season, I maxed out my line of credit and took out a home equity loan to provide a buffer for periods when I couldn't pay myself.

Lesson Learned: Despite believing the only way to work less was to hire people to do the work, I discovered that my life, even at the practice level, was much simpler and had much less anxiety without staff. I never went without a paycheck before I had a team there to "help" me.

Likewise, when examining the earnings leveragability in a business, the ownership style also contributes to the compensation (or, in business, we say pricing) model. For example, when you are an employee of a business, you are compensated for your labor (inputs). The only way to increase your earnings is by laboring more (working more hours). In an employee-owned, and manager-owned business, this is especially true as the business owners tends to price based on the age-old tradition of labor power. In these types of businesses, the product (or result) of the labor is stripped away, and the business owns it, free to determine the time and conditions it uses the labor. By charging for labor, one can rarely experience leverage, as the labor is used up in the process.

In an investor-owned business, however, a different pricing model is used. Going back to Finley's analysis, the investor sells the product, not the labor. As such, he has produced this product (result) in his own time and under his own conditions of work. In an investor-owned business, one does price based not on time but on the value he creates. Thus, leverage can be created as earnings are not directly in proportion to the time it takes to create value. Unlike employee- and manager-owned businesses, when pricing based on value, to increase earnings, it is not necessary to increase time or labor, but instead to increase value created.

Do you know which business ownership type you are currently operating? Are you purposefully planning to grow your business to function differently? Here is where self-assessment comes into play. Briefly think about your day-to-day functions: How much of a hands-on role are you required to have in order for your business to thrive? If something happens to you, if you aren't there, will the business continue to produce income?

Dominique's Story

Five years into my CPA practice, I was running a manager-owned business. I had some systems and reliable staff members, but I certainly didn't have the freedom that owning a business was supposed to bring. I had to examine my deficiencies that were holding me back from becoming a bona fide investor-owned business. I had no choice but to make some serious changes in my practice. My first instinct was that perhaps I was not cut out for being the owner of a tax business. Yet, this idea didn't feel satisfying. There were many things I loved about my work, and I hated the idea of losing the things I enjoyed most in my business. Still, feeling stuck and frustrated was not a state in which I wanted to reside. I reverted to a "pros and cons" list. Filling the "pros" side were planning, problem-solving, and relationships. A much longer list filled the "cons" side: everything else in my company. The situation looked hopeless. I recognized all the things I loved doing in my business generated no income! I offered problem-solving and tax advice connected to the compliance duties, which didn't pay enough because I charged based on time. As I daydreamed about how to improve the situation, I began to wonder, "If I could somehow get paid well for only the things I love to do, that would be amazing!"

Lesson Learned: Before exiting a negative situation, be sure to assess the entire loss. You just might be throwing away some "pros" along with the "cons."

How Much Is Owning a Tax Practice Costing You?

In the end, you may realize that you have created the worst kind of job and hired yourself to carry it out. You may have created a job with an awful boss who makes you work constantly, under stressful conditions, with a never-ending "to-do" list. Kiss your spouse, kids, friends, and dog goodbye for most of the year as you go underground to sign off on mountains of paperwork. You'll be sure to earn above minimum wage, but you'll likely be unhappy with your "real" hourly rate (See figure 1.1). Your retirement benefits leave much to be desired as well. In fact, you'll only end up with about one year's worth of revenue when you sell the firm, which hopefully will be enough to last through your golden years.

This chapter may have gotten you started to consider your current situation. Owning a job is not all it's cracked up to be. In fact, I'd say it's much worse than being gainfully employed with seemingly secure income, benefits, and a quitting time. If you find yourself in this same situation, there is light at the end of the tunnel, and it starts by ending your habit of trading time for dollars. We'll explore other aspects of this as we continue this journey.

Chapter One in Review

- There is a longstanding practice of valuing compensation based on labor-time. In this model, the product or result is stripped away from the labor necessary to create it, and it is not considered in the valuation.
- We often lose sight of the original motivations for starting a business—are you experiencing your ideals?
- Don't forget about the other "costs" of owning a business such as relationship issues, health problems, and impact on other life goals or opportunities.
- There are three styles of business ownership: employee-owned, manager-owned, and investor-owned.
- Leverage is nearly impossible to create when pricing based on time, but easy to create when pricing based on products or value.

CHAPTER 2

Get Paid for Your Expertise: Value-Pricing Your Services

Tax Returns

An Accountant's Perception versus a Client's Perception

In most service relationships, the seller and the buyer possess two different opinions on the same subject. This rings true in the accountant–taxpayer relationship. I'd like to dispel a couple of myths, and I want to give you a little test.

The exercise I'm going to ask you to participate in is called "The Price is Right." The intent is to reveal how much you would charge a client for the tax return described in Figure 2.1.

Figure 2.1 How Much Do You Really Earn?

Form 1040 – 5 dependent children

Schedule A

Schedule C – Reporting $17,000 in net income

Form 8283 with one donation of household goods

Figure 2.1 shows a standard 1040 tax return form, and this particular taxpayer has five dependent children. In addition to having a Schedule A, he has a Schedule C, which reveals $17,000 in income. Also, the taxpayer has a charitable donation schedule. What I'd like for you to do is develop a fee for preparing this tax return. Be honest here. What would you charge a client for the type of tax return seen in Figure 2.1?

Remember, the amount you choose doesn't represent what you *want* to charge—it represents what you *would* charge. The pricing options are:

- $0–$300
- $301–$500
- $501–$750, or
- over $750

In a recent survey, The American Institute of Certified Tax Coaches (AICTC) polled tax business owners on how much they would charge for this exact 1040 tax return. Out of those polled, 28% claimed they would charge less than $300, 44% asserted they would charge anywhere from $301 to $500, 11% said they would charge between $501 to $750, and 17% of -tax business owners polled revealed they would charge over $750. When the respondents were asked to specify their price, the poll results revealed the average desired fee was $350. The lowest price quoted in this survey was $107, whereas the highest was $850.

According to recent results from the National Association of Tax Preparers (NATP) survey, the national average asking price is $508 for a similar tax return. Eighty percent of the respondents in the NATP survey are Certified Public Accountants (CPAs). Do the results surprise you? Pricing truly is the Loch Ness Monster of the tax profession. If there is a "going rate" for a tax return such as the one shown in Figure 2.1, how is it possible to have such a large gap between the highest fee of $850 and the lowest fee of just $107 for the same exact return? This demonstrates the subjectivity of pricing tax returns.

Exactly how do most tax accountants develop their pricing? Do you look to others in the business and modify it? Do you study industry surveys? Perhaps you anticipate what the public will pay and apply that to your pricing structure. Whichever method you choose, it's clear that the concept of industry-standard pricing is an illusion.

There are always more ways of looking at things. In the tax profession, the two that matter most are the accountant's perception, and the client's perception.

Let's discuss pricing from your point of view. The following are a few common viewpoints of tax professionals:

- I am the best at what I do; my prices should reflect that.
- I bring a wealth of experience and knowledge to my clients; I should charge more.

On the other hand, clients have their own viewpoints, including the following:

- I can pay any accountant to prepare my tax return; they are all the same.
- There's really not much to tax prep; just put numbers on a form and you're done.
- There is a market rate for preparing a tax return.

As you may have guessed, the respective viewpoints from both sides contradict one another.

As tax professionals, we believe and argue that we are the best at what we do. We understand the time, effort, and expertise that go into tax law, and we feel that our time is more valuable than software or retail preparation stores. The clients think that they are paying us to simply prepare a form, and that accountants are a dime a dozen.

The second viewpoint is that tax professionals think about the wealth of experience and knowledge they bring to the table when deciding on a "fair" price, while the clients think there is a standard rate. The truth is consumers generally don't understand the requirements of our work. Because of this, the only thing they can use as a comparative feature is price When we consider this with the centuries-old idea of valuing compensation based on labor, and the industry model of hourly billing, the public wants us to compete with each other based on price. This competition, coupled with new technology for "do-it-yourselfers," leaves tax pros charging less-than-desirable fees.

Seeking to increase earnings, most practitioners take on higher volumes of returns to "get paid what you're worth." Practitioners want to earn the kind of money that you feel that you're worth, and the only way to do that when you're making such little money per return is to take on additional clients. In fact, I've met dozens of practitioners who personally prepare over 1,000 tax returns each season. Now that's high volume! It's an extraordinary amount of work. This logic is counterproductive to your ultimate goal of getting paid what you're worth. To remain competitive, instead of earning the dollar value you desire for each tax return, you're settling for less money per return. So, in essence, you're getting paid less more often than when you began.

The key to getting paid what you're worth without doing thousands of tax returns is to change your clients' viewpoint that there is a going rate and that they can pay any accountant to do the job. If people truly understand the value that they receive from you, they will not let price get in the way of their choice of accountants.

Examining other industries is key in illustrating this concept. For example, consider how doctors bill their patients. Depending on the procedure, physicians make thousands of dollars per minute in actuality. Most of the time, the patients are satisfied with paying that kind of money because of the way physicians demonstrate their value to their patients.

Let's say a woman is visiting the doctor because she needs surgery for kidney stones, a very painful ailment. On one hand, the doctor could present the cost as a billing rate by the minute, which is the equivalent to an accountant billing by the hour. The patient probably won't be too happy with that figure, and she's most likely going to shop around for the going rate, or for what she thinks is a fair rate for the surgery. Have you ever received this reaction when you quoted your fees to prospective clients? You likely have. Pricing in this way focuses the consumer's attention on the inputs of the process. In a way, you are communicating that the inputs (or time spent) is the most important part of the transaction. In reality, the effort it takes to complete an engagement is not the most important part of the transaction. Yet, due to tradition, most accountants are conditioned to believe that the billable hour is the most important contribution we can make to the firm. Employees are rewarded for generating lots of billable hours, and larger firms are even valued more for it.

On the other hand, the doctor refrains from talking about rates. Instead, he explains how he can relieve his patient's pain. In doing this, the doctor demonstrates his value without talking about money or time. Let's say he then tells her that relieving her pain is only going to cost around $10,000. By focusing on the value brought to the patient in the form of pain relief, physicians successfully get paid their worth. Directing customers' attention to the value you bring creates a relationship built on respect, trust, and value. Arguably, these elements are the most important parts of any accounting transaction.

This leads to a discussion about trading time for dollars because time is really a commodity. If you think that you don't sell time, I want you to think again. You may not actually sell time, but the services take time to deliver, and charging by the hour limits your earnings because your earning potential is tied to a limited resource. There are only 24 hours in a day; there simply is no way around it. This is why most accountants try to resolve the earnings-limitation problem by servicing even more customers.

If you're saying to yourself, "I already charge a flat fee for a tax return," I have to tell you that if you develop that fee based on how long it takes you to complete the tax return, you're actually selling time. Time is a limited resource, and until there are more billable hours in a month, you will always experience a ceiling on your earnings. Likewise, trading time for dollars will ensure that your income relies on your ability to produce. Raising your rates is an option, but remember clients believe in the concept of a going rate. Because of this viewpoint, raising your rates without additional value will not work for an extended amount of time. It is only a matter of time before taxpayers feel they are paying more than everyone else. Additionally, there is a funny thing about raising prices: If you want to charge them more, people actually expect more for it. For a practitioner who is already maxed out, burned out, and stressed out, providing more work won't solve the problem!

Creating Invoices for Value

A typical invoice from the average accounting practice traditionally displays an hourly billing rate. Let's say that after one hour of research, the invoice shows $195. This rate isn't necessarily bad, but how do you think the client feels about it? Take a look at Figure 2.2.

Figure 2.2

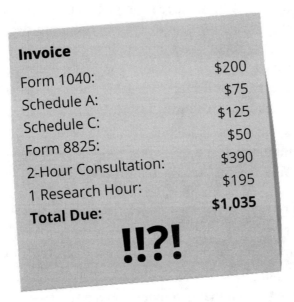

If you include the hourly rates on your invoices, what kind of response do you get from your clients? Imagine you create an invoice to prepare a form, and you've broken down every task with your hourly rates. When you highlight every detail of the hourly rate, people generally feel like they're overpaying. Clients may refute your charges, claiming

- "I don't remember consulting with you for two hours."
- "Why did you need an hour to research? Shouldn't you know that already?"
- "Did it really take you all that time to prepare my return?" or
- "I could have just done my return myself."

Maybe you're already familiar with responses like these. Perhaps you're at a point where you anticipate taxpayers responding in such a manner. It's a vicious cycle, but I want to show you an alternative to your current billing method. What I call the "value invoice" is shown in Figure 2.3.

Figure 2.3 The Value Invoice

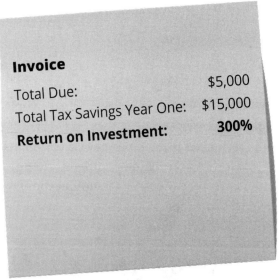

Figure 2.3 is an example of a value invoice for the same work performed in the previous example. As you can see, the price difference in the two examples is almost $4,000. As far as time goes, however, assuming it still took you the same amount of time to do this work, the value-based invoice makes no mention of time or hourly rates. If you think about it in terms of what is most meaningful in a customer transaction (respect, trust, and value), the amount of time spent on the engagement is irrelevant. In fact, the description of the tax return is not present at all. You're not selling time in the value-based invoice. Yet, the inputs or efforts are exactly the same in both scenarios. You've done the same research that you charged $195 per hour, in the first example.

Examining the product, or results, you actually saved the client $15,000. Thus, in the second example, your invoice presents your fee in addition to the value that you created in the engagement; in this scenario, the value is the tax savings of $15,000. The reaction of the client in this situation is really quite different than when presenting hourly rates. By placing the importance on the value of your work, the amount you're charging becomes irrelevant. The difference between the two types of invoices is where you are directing your clients' focus. When you're focusing on the value that you bring to the relationship, you change the perception of what you are being paid to do. Clients begin to feel that perhaps they cannot get similar services elsewhere, and they are forced to make a comparison on something other than price, and that is value.

Finally, the argumentativeness of the engagement is completely different in a value-pricing model as compared to pricing based on time. Since your efforts remain relatively unseen, when people are unhappy with the price of a product or service, they may try to argue about it. You've probably experienced these types of disagreements from time to time. Have you ever found yourself defending how long you spent on a project because the customer is calling it into question? When examining value, particularly financial value created through tax work, there isn't a lot to argue. If the tax liability is lower after your work, the taxpayer can either see the value or he cannot. While we can't connect or use the tax results as a factor of our fees ethically, there isn't really much left to argue about at the end of an engagement priced on value. (Some of this is due to the timing of the pricing discussion, which I'll discuss later in this book.)

Getting Paid Based on Value

The purpose of this book is to teach you how to get paid for the value of your worth. As I discussed in the last section, value pricing really begins by highlighting your expertise. The first step is to fully understand that value yourself. Do you believe you offer something of value? What do people find most valuable about the work that you do?

These questions can be difficult to answer if you don't believe the work you are doing is important. As accountants, we understand the importance of meeting the compliance requirements of the IRS and other governmental authorities. But without experience and expertise, it is difficult for the public to place a value on our work.

So, if the public does not see value in the preparation of forms, what value do we actually offer customers? It may be necessary to evaluate your core product offerings to identify the worth of your services. Do you offer products and services that are unique to the market? These services may vary from business coaching, to outsourced CFO work, to financial assistance. Still, calculating the precise monetary value of the work is difficult.

For this reason, tax planning lends itself especially well to value-based pricing. The reason is simple: when your ideas and expertise create savings for people, that money is real and demonstrable. For example, if you suggest to a sole proprietor that he or she can save money if the business is run as an S corporation, his/her bank account increases by the amount of employment taxes saved on the profits taken as a distribution. Tax planning allows you to show the world the value of your work in dollars and cents.

In a sense, you are selling dollars, not time. A taxpayer can pay you for an hour of your time, or they can pay you to lower their taxes by $15,000 per year. Which option do you think is more attractive?

Most tax professionals offer what I refer to as "tax tips" as a means of tax planning. Some consider fall tax projections of their anticipated tax liability as tax planning. Both can result in tax reduction for clients, but how you position these services changes the perception of the value they create. When you offer solutions that slash a customer's tax bill, how do you communicate that to them? Do you routinely promote this value in your marketing, sales presentations, and invoicing?

When you actively promote the benefits of your expertise, specifically the financial benefits of working with you, you instantly convey why someone should want to pay top dollar to work with you. Why, then, do most tax accountants not offer formal tax planning?

The answer is that the traditional accounting model does not give you enough room to allow you to work proactively. Simply stated, we are talking about working proactively versus reactively.

As I've shared with you here, most accountants face the employee-owned business trap. That is, they take on high volumes of work in an effort to get paid what they're worth. Ordinarily, this works, provided the high volumes of people don't all require personal services at the same time. Yet in tax, everyone has the same deadlines. The result is an endless list of unfinished work, and with the increasing rate of IRS correspondence, the situation worsens.

Perhaps you'd like to be able to work proactively with your clients, but your current schedule doesn't allow time for that. Most accountants provide reactive service. That is, when the taxpayer requests services, you provide them. But how often do you proactively reach out and offer services during the rest of the year?

If your long-term schedule is largely undetermined because it is based on the needs of your clients, this may indicate you work reactively versus proactively. If you're not sure how your day is going to go until you come into the office, you run a reactive business. Perhaps you receive IRS notices or client requests you need to respond to. Do you find yourself changing your priorities to fit in these client "emergencies?" Working proactively will change your relationship with your clients. In reality, IRS notices, client requests, and even audits include time to prepare. Working proactively, on your terms for all work in your office, will change the way you do business.

Consider again, the ancient economic principle of the worker. He or she is not in control of their time and effort, but this is owned by the business to be used as desired. You may want to work more proactively with your clients, but the demands of your business won't allow you the time you need for this type of work.

Meeting with your customers at your request throughout the year to identify and meet their needs is proactive work. When you sit down for pre-planned consultations, it provides the chance to do real planning; taking advantage of opportunities available before transactions take place. Routinely reviewing your work files and searching for tax-reduction opportunities is proactive work—it is valuable in real dollars to taxpayers.

I talked previously about eliminating long hours and low prices, and how important presenting your value to the client is. When you're creating leverage through value pricing, you can afford to spend more time in your work creating value. Additionally, you have the option to work with fewer clients, and that frees up your schedule to deliver the proactive services that people really want. Working proactively grants you the freedom that owning a business is supposed to bring you.

Once you realize your value and start getting paid what you're truly worth, a domino effect will occur. Increasing your income can change a lot of things for you. When you begin to charge for your expertise, and you increase your prices, you can do what you need to begin owning your business as an investor, such as recruiting and retaining top support staff for your business. A funny thing happens when you change the focus of your products and services. When your entire team is focused on creating the ultimate value for your clients rather than the number of billable hours, the quality of the work improves. Again, the goal of owning a tax practice is to give you enough free time to work on your business instead of in it as an employee. Providing your team with more clarity on their focus will free you up to actually own the business as an investor.

Another benefit of highlighting your expertise is that you completely eliminate your competition. Accountants know that not all tax professionals are the same. Unfortunately, the public doesn't know this. The truth is, most taxpayers view you and your competitors as the same, as doing the same work, whether or not you're providing the same service. Taxpayers do apples-to-apples comparisons, and no matter how good you are, you and your competitors are really both apples. These comparisons make it hard for you to charge what you're really worth because people can always find someone who's faster, cheaper, and more convenient—someone who doesn't value their time as much as you do—making it impossible for you to justify premium fees.

How can you avoid the apples-to-apples comparison? You need to offer something new and different. Give taxpayers what they really want—tax reduction—instead of only something that they need. True tax planning means giving your clients specific strategies: Telling them what to do, how to do it, and when to do it to cut their bottom-line tax bill. Don't include this as part of a tax return—treat it as a separate service and price it as a separate service. Call your client in as a separate engagement to work on tax planning, so that you can eliminate your competition.

When your client sees that you deliver ways to pay less in tax, this establishes a difference between what you and your competitors have to offer. Now you're not seen as an apple in a multitude of apples—you now stand out as an orange, and you can use this advantage to charge for your value, which translates to premium fees. Taxpayers don't care what your competition charges if your competitors don't offer the kind of value you bring. In fact, many times over the years, I've had prospective customers contact my competitors asking what kind of tax savings they could offer. I have to chuckle to myself imagining how my competition answered these types of inquiries.

Focusing on the value that you deliver reinforces your worth; your clients are more loyal. They do business on your terms, and they are more organized throughout the year, making your job easier. They don't procrastinate but show a willingness to help. They don't judge you for taking three weeks off in the summer because they perceive you as delivering something that they can't get anywhere else. They respect the way you run your business, and they want to refer people they care about, so that they, too, can save money.

National Association of Tax Preparers Statistics

Earlier, I mentioned the NATP in regard to pricing the preparation of a tax return. I want to share the remainder of the NATP survey with you, so you can gauge where you are in your own tax practice compared to accountants all over the country.

The typical independent accountant

- is a 57-year-old male
- has been in practice for 25 years
- has at least a four-year college education
- is a sole proprietor

The typical practice

- operates as a sole proprietorship
- has an annual gross practice income of $246,176
- has a net income of $84,790
- has four full-time employees
- has two part-time employees
- has three seasonal employees
- has two full-time principals/partners, when in a partnership
- processes 157 non-itemized 1040s annually
- processes 293 itemized Schedule A 1040s annually
- derives 60 percent of gross income from the preparation of federal/state tax returns
- currently offers electronic filing to clients and charges $24 for the service
- charges an hourly fee of $129 to represent clients before IRS
- has not seen an increase in audits over the past year
- has e-filed two-thirds of all 1040s
- uses personal interviews to collect data from clients
- allocates 40 percent of total expenses to salaries/benefits
- allocates 11 percent of annual expenses for technology products.

The typical firm charges an average of

- $58 for a Form 940 (federal unemployment)
- $129 for preparation of a Form 1040, not itemized
- $229 for an itemized Form 1040

- $415 for preparation of Form 1041 (fiduciary)
- $488 for preparation of a Form 5500 (pension/profit-sharing plans)
- $551 for a Form 1065 (partnership)
- $584 for a Form 990 (tax exempt)
- $665 for a Form 1120S (S corporation)
- $692 for a Form 1120 (corporation)

Typical—or average—fees (hourly):

- Payroll-preparation services: $75
- Write-up work: $84
- Presentation of financial statements: $110
- Elder-care services: $111
- Management advisory service fees: $127
- Tax services: $128
- Audit of financial statements: $135
- Estate-financial-planning services: $138

The typical firm

- Bills at the end of the job (60%)
- Accepts credit card payments (30%)
- Charges interest on past-due accounts (23%)
- Utilizes progress billing (23%)
- Itemizes charges for copies, faxes, deliveries, phone calls, etc. (17%)
- Requests a percentage of payment at the time of engagement letter (10%)

Common Traps

1. **Not routinely assessing your business to make sure it is on the right track.**

   "Going with the flow" not only leads to chaos, it also makes you lose sight of why you started your business, and what you hoped to achieve from running a practice. Having a lack of vision or an unclear goal is the easiest way to ensure things will never change. Where you currently find yourself is most likely where you will be next year, five years from now, and beyond.

   Implementing systems and methods can help you stay on track in your daily and even yearly routines. Use a "health checkup" method regularly to assess your business—I'll discuss this further in Chapter 9.

2. **Forgetting the reason(s) you started a tax practice in the first place.**

   Every entrepreneur had specific goals in mind when they started their own business. Working yourself to the bone and not getting paid what you're worth certainly was not one of those goals. Re-identify the goals you had when you started your practice. If you can honestly assess your current business and conclude that your short- and long-term goals are not being met, you need to make changes.

3. **Basing your totals on an annual total instead of an hourly rate.**

   Looking at your gross revenues may appeal to you, but the truth is that after you subtract overhead and add in the number of hours you actually worked, you may not be happy with the result. To appropriately determine your desired income, first plan your lifestyle and then calculate the costs to support it. Next, calculate the number of clients you can afford the time to work proactively with. This indicates the average fees per client you need to secure to provide the lifestyle you desire. Knowing your hourly rate determines the value you are receiving from your business, and clients knowing their savings determine the value they are receiving from choosing you as a tax planner. Also, don't forget to include the "non-monetary" costs of your business in your calculations; opportunity costs often create the biggest deficits.

4. **Misunderstanding the clients' perception.**

   There are two sides to every story: you know the amount you're charging your clients is fair, while your clients want to get the best services possible at the best rate available. The reality is that your clients' opinions of your services are very important. If your client feels that he or she can get the same services for the same fee elsewhere, you'll inevitably become obsolete. The key is to demonstrate to your clients exactly what you're worth, so they'll value your services and pay you accordingly.

5. **Charging fees based on your competitors' fees.**

   As mentioned in this chapter, most clients believe there is a going rate for preparing tax returns. However, this is a myth. Not all accountants are the same. Connecting your fees to a competitor's prices shifts the control of one of the most important aspects of your business: pricing. Never give control of your business to someone who has no interest in your vision. No one can define your worth except you.

6. **Working reactively rather than proactively.**

   Consider this metaphor: You're a professional baseball player up at bat. Waiting for the perfect pitch to cross the plate is reactive; going after pitches and putting the ball in play is proactive. Which option is going to make the fans happier? Proactive behavior proves to your clients that you're worth what you're getting paid—it demonstrates your value. Remember, an important step toward changing your clients' perception of your worth is removing their apples-to-apples comparison and showing them that you're unique—an orange that can't be compared to an apple—because you offer a different service and do so proactively and with better results.

Did You Know?

When polled by AICTC:

- 5 percent of tax business owners indicated that they charge for services by form; 65 percent charge by an hourly rate; 25 percent charge fees based on a time-estimated flat rate; and 1 percent based charges on competitors' prices.
- While 15 percent of respondents recognized staff members as reliable, 40 percent maintained that their staff has room for improvement, and 35 percent of accountants revealed that they do not have a support staff.

Complimentary Pricing Essentials Tool Kit

Includes:

Worksheets from this book

Price Increase Announcement Template

Price Increase Package Opt-In Certificate Template

Price Offer Opt-Out Certificate Template

Audit Protection Package Profit Analyzer

Get Paid What You're Worth Home Video Course

Just visit www.GetPaidForYourWorth.com

CHAPTER 3

Value-Pricing: Good for Your Clients—and You

Examining other industries generally leads to creativity and ideas for improvement in your own business. So far, we've looked at how the medical profession uses value pricing so successfully that the public accepts it and continuously generates programs to afford the costs (think public health care, insurance, etc.).

Another component to consider in establishing your pricing model is ethical responsibilities. Referring to the medical profession, there may not be another profession with so much responsibility, liability, and regulation. Looking at these considerations in the context of pricing, it is easy to see why physicians need to charge so much: they have too much to cover in their professional responsibilities, and they need adequate revenues to allow for due care.

In comparison, the tax profession also has great responsibilities. Generally covered under Circular 230, tax professionals have regulations to practice before the IRS, and non-compliance leads to steep penalties. While these regulations govern how tax professionals render advice, represent clients before the IRS, and carry out responsibilities in tax return filings, this guidance does not address professional responsibility as it relates to the requirement of proactive advice. That is, tax pros are not required under the law to make recommendations to the client that lead to more favorable tax outcomes. There is simply no standard or requirement, nor any imposed penalties for failing to act proactively to help your clients.

It is easy to see why this is the case. Imagine the regulations it would require. Currently, anyone can act as a tax professional and prepare tax returns. How exactly would the government enforce such a requirement if there is no current requirement for licensing to prepare a tax return?[1]

However, simply because the law does not require this proactive advice does not mean that we, as professionals, can't adopt our own definition of professional responsibility when it comes to offering advice that would save taxpayers from paying taxes they do not have to pay. The problem with this individual set of ethics is that it would become virtually impossible to deliver this kind of service at "industry pricing" and still remain profitable. Consider how much additional time each case would require if you had to carefully examine the situation and run projections to determine tax-reduction strategies—is that possible with average fees under $1,000? I've already established the destructive cycle tax professionals experience just from offering tax-preparation services under ineffective pricing models. Adding more services included with low-priced tax return preparation would sabotage an already fragile business. Imagine the level of burnout you would feel.

How Much Are You Costing Your Clients?

Since most professionals don't adequately charge for planning, and since we don't have a regulatory duty to provide tax-reduction advice, many tax professionals simply don't do tax planning at all. With this in mind, it makes you wonder how much you might be injuring your clients by not offering this service.

Can you imagine having that conversation—letting someone know what you've missed in tax-saving opportunities over the years? The AICTC surveys tax planners across the country and has surmised that the average small-business owner wastes about $15,000 per year in taxes

---

[1] In January 2013, the Internal Revenue Service announced that it was suspending the RTRP program because of a ruling by a district court that issued an order prohibiting the IRS from enforcing the regulatory requirements for registered tax return preparers.

they simply do not have to pay. This occurs either because they do not receive tax-planning services, or they receive bad advice. With this in mind, you must ask yourself how much you have cost taxpayers by not providing tax-planning services. No doubt, it's a frightening thought.

Dominique's Story

Early in my career, I would typically offer "tax tips" to my clients when we would meet to discuss their tax returns. I enjoyed being able to provide helpful advice and relief from the aggravation of high taxes. I started to notice, however, that a lot of people failed to take my advice. I suppose, in most instances, I never took the time to follow up and see if they ever implemented my ideas. I came to realize that I seemed to be offering the same advice year after year, which was a pretty good indication that people were not using my ideas.

When I began charging separately for tax-planning services, I was terrified at the thought of presenting this to my existing clients. I feared their reaction and wondered if they would be upset that I had not made these recommendations sooner. This is a common concern among newly certified tax planners. In my experience, people are so happy that I'm able to help them that they don't recognize that they could have been using these ideas much earlier in our relationship. The truth is, it is possible for people to feel upset about the time they were not benefitting from this service. Perhaps they might hold their advisor responsible, but in my own professional responsibility, I hold myself responsible for bringing this to taxpayers' attention despite being fearful of their reaction.

In reality, my clients were overjoyed to keep more of their income and happily paid increased costs—they saw my fees as a bargain. And I saw my responsibility to bring this important work to them as soon as I realized it rather than not at all.

Lesson Learned: It's better to continuously improve your services even if it means facing a fear.

Tracy's Story

Tracy had been in business 15 years before getting certified in tax planning. She had developed a comfortable, successful business. Her gross revenues were about 1 million per year, and she employed a healthy staff of seven. As a CPA, Tracy saw the need for tax planning and incorporated it regularly into her business. Each year, her more complex clients saw the value in what she was doing, which was running projections and offering ideas to reduce tax bills. She followed the industry model of billing hourly for this work and typically would spend about two to three hours on each project, including the time to meet with her clients.

When Tracy learned about the tax-planning certification, she was interested in learning more ways she could offer value to her clients; she was eager to identify additional techniques to work with loopholes and deductions. After the first day of training, Tracy was intrigued by the idea of value-based pricing, but wondered how she might ever change from billing $600 to $700 per plan to billing $5,000 or more for the same two to three hours of work. She feared what her clients might think, but identified with the concept of value pricing and believed it could completely change her income possibilities.

By the second day of training, Tracy started realizing precisely how much money she had been helping her clients keep over the years, and it all began to make sense. Helping her clients grow their wealth by six and even seven figures throughout their relationship really had nothing to do with how much time it took her to accomplish the work. She also knew that the amount of time she spent with each client was not the only time she spent developing her expertise and skills in this area. Just like a doctor, Tracy invested years of schooling and time honing her experience to be able to apply these tax-planning strategies to each client's unique circumstances—and she deserved to be paid for this work.

> Returning home from this discovery, Tracy planned a new way of operating her business, and that decision has proved profitable. Now, Tracy regularly communicates her value to her clients, and they happily pay 10 times or more in fees, knowing they are in good hands.
>
> **Lesson Learned:** Getting paid for the work you're doing right now does not always represent the work it took to prepare you for this moment.

Is Tax Planning Optional?

One of the problems with offering tax planning as an additional service without communicating its value is that taxpayers don't understand the work we do. Think about this concept: People come to us for the numbers. How would they ever know that our expertise saves them thousands of dollars each year unless we showed them that calculation? And since it is difficult to identify the value without assistance from their "numbers person," most people view this service as optional.

Have you ever offered a tax-planning session and received a reply such as, "No, I think I am OK for now," or "Isn't that part of the work you already do?" The only reason someone would decline a service that provides them more cash is if the cost outweighs the benefits, or if they don't understand the benefits. Consider this analogy: If you could frequent a business that offered you discounted money, say, $10,000 at a cost of $2,500, would you buy its services? Of course you would, assuming it is legal U.S. currency. Yet, people often decline additional services that essentially offer this exact benefit. The only logical explanation is that the individual doesn't understand the offer and the value of the benefit; they don't understand that if they pay you for this work, their bank account will grow.

Much of this misunderstanding has to do with an ignorance towards the tax system. There is much confusion around a tax refund, estimated tax payments, withholding, self-employment, and other taxes. Many people don't realize that an income tax refund is a refund of their own money—there are people in this country who still think a tax refund is free money from the government. Therefore, when you communicate about tax savings or tax reductions, it's difficult for the client to see that this is indeed real money—that the conclusion of the engagement will result in a larger bank account.

Making the assumption that people understand the value of the work we do is an expensive mistake. But it has an easy fix: With every engagement, be sure to communicate the exact value of the work you are doing—and quote your fee next to that statement. For example, if I identify a method for the client to use income shifting and multiple entities in their business that saves them $30,000 each year in taxes, I might say something like this:

> "Mr. Green, I'm glad you came in today, because I have some ideas that can save you about $30,000 off your tax bill each year from now on. This means you may even be able to skip your third-quarter estimated tax payment. The best news is it's only going to cost you $10,000 to implement the idea! Can you come in this week to review it?"

I will discuss more about developing your pricing structure later in this book, but let's examine the structure of this statement to Mr. Green. First, I took ownership of the solution to Mr. Green's tax problem ("I have some ideas that can save you…"). Next, I quantified the monetary benefit of my work ("that can save you about $30,000 each year in taxes…"). Finally, I communicated my price for this work at the same time, so that I positioned my cost along with the value of working with me ("It's only going to cost you $10,000 to implement the idea!"). Now Mr. Green understands my value and does not view that value as coming from the amount of time it took me to develop the ideas.

Using a more traditional model of billing, a conversation with Mr. Green might sound something like this:

> "Mr. Green, it's time for your fall tax-planning meeting. We really need to do this before your next estimated tax payment

is due, and I'm running out of time in my schedule. Can you come in next week to meet?"

In the traditional model of billing, you would meet with Mr. Green and communicate the amount of his quarterly estimated tax payment and send him a bill for about two to three hours of time multiplied by your hourly billing rate. You may or may not notice the opportunity for Mr. Green to reduce his tax bill since you are busy moving on to the next project on your to-do list. And even if you do, you most likely fail to let Mr. Green know how much you've helped him add to his bank account this year.

One of the best benefits of value pricing is that you can show people how to get your service for free! (Even if the price is 10 times higher than you've ever charged.) Under the traditional billing model, people view accounting fees as a cost of doing business. It's tough to show a return on investment for a tax-preparation fee. Instead, communicating the tax savings you help create for people allows you to position your fees as an investment. By lowering someone's tax bill, it's as if you don't cost them anything at all!

Value Billing Provides More Certainty for Clients

I'll discuss later how to change the timing of your billing to automated monthly billing, but for now, let's examine how value-based pricing provides more certainty for taxpayers.

To explain this subject, I like to look at attorneys as an example of client frustration with hourly billing. Most attorneys charge for their work using an hourly billing model. Have you ever cut your conversation with an attorney short because you worried about the size of your bill? I know I've watched the clock during my conversations with my lawyer and even cut out small talk for fear of receiving a four-figure invoice for a simple telephone conversation or email. Our clients frequently do the same thing. This leads to a more reactive approach to tax work.

Most people know they should consult with their accountant when they make a major financial transaction (purchasing a home, making an investment, starting a business), but most don't, and I propose it's because of both the uncertainty about the cost of the consult as well as the lack of responsiveness of the tax professional.

While tax pros are busy surviving their huge workload, they are not proactively reaching out to people because of the cost in time, and at the same time people are not reaching out to their advisors. This leads to a reactive work structure. It's impossible to change history, and many tax-reduction opportunities are lost simply because advisors learn about transactions after they take place. Without the chance to properly structure the opportunity, this model causes wasted tax monies. It's an expensive way of working together! Yet, when you value-bill and work with less clients in a better way, people understand the cost and the benefit of working with you. In turn, you have the time available to proactively work in advance of transactions, and you can advise the best course of action for an optimal tax position. Open, two-way communication exists, and a trusting, loyal relationship ensues.

Better advice, lower taxes, more certainty in costs, and a return on investment are all incredible benefits people receive when working under a value-based pricing agreement. Likewise, the tax professional enjoys higher profits, better client relationships, less stress, and more certainty in scheduling and in needed resources using value-based pricing. In short, value pricing creates a win-win for everyone involved!

CHAPTER 4

How to Use Leverage and Scale a Tax Business

No matter how much we will it to happen, there will never be more than 24 hours in a day. This puts a limit on your earning potential because you are trading your time for dollars. How does the traditional tax industry try to get around this limitation? By hiring more people! Yet, if you think about it, each new hire is also billing for time—and also has just 24 hours in a day. No matter how many people you plug into the equation, you will always be limited in your earning potential. Perhaps this is why, on average, more than 80 percent of tax professionals earn just $150,000 per year.

When doing hourly billing, the only way to increase your earnings is to increase the billing rate. Yet, as I've established earlier in this book, the public has a certain expectation about the "going rate" for tax services and generally expect more when required to pay more. That perception seems to make it impossible to raise your rates above what is considered the standard rates. We've seen this in recent times when the Big 4 accounting firms began losing customers who were becoming more sensitive toward the high hourly rates: The perception that bigger firms were providing better service that justified higher fees began to diminish as the economy declined.

It's important to consider all the sources of "competition" that define the going rate. Today, it is easier and cheaper than ever to get tax assistance, including free online resources and smartphone apps that let taxpayers file their taxes on the go. Even the IRS has entered the game by offering free e-filing services. From the public's standpoint, these are all viable options. Given the amount of free and low-cost help available, it's no surprise that people expect low-cost options when seeking help with tax needs. This puts pressure on advisors to set their hourly rates as low as possible to remain competitive.

A pitfall exists when a business owner attempts to increase profit margins by hiring low-cost staff: along with lower costs come lower competencies. Managing the risk of more errors requires even more of the owner's time—which often leads to lower profit margins than without staff! I'm sure you've experienced this situation before: actually losing money on engagements where your team made mistakes that required you to put significant time into re-doing the work or repairing the problem. Often, it would have been more profitable to do the work yourself, without the "help" of your employees.

It's difficult to develop a plan to scale your business without room in the profit margins to afford additional technology and human resources. Again, this is why more than 80 percent of tax businesses are stuck at a limited size.

Value-based pricing provides a solution not only to the hourly pricing problem, but also to the scaling problem. Disconnecting your value from the amount of time a project requires allows you to increase the price of your services. In turn, your profit margins increase and allow room for you to hire more experienced help and dramatically grow the business. Creating better margins makes room to provide better, more proactive services, which increases demand for your services. Applying economic principles, greater demand causes higher pressure on price, driving them up and making your business more profitable.

When you bill hourly, it's impossible to use leverage to improve your profits. As discussed previously in this book, each hour billed is used up in labor fulfilling the service. If you want to optimize your income potential, most successful businesses leverage their operations by using fixed costs when revenues are variable. This allows you to create greater profit margins while keeping your costs constant. As long as your income and your costs (i.e., hourly wages) are a variable of the time factor,, the only way you can improve profits is to raise fees; however, even raising fees will not improve margins. In essence, your profit percentage will always remain the same when both revenues and costs are tied to work hours.

In contrast, value-based pricing abstracts revenues from labor hours, while wages remain a fixed cost. This allows you to leverage these costs: the higher your fees increase, the greater your profit margins improve, and the business growth can grow exponentially.

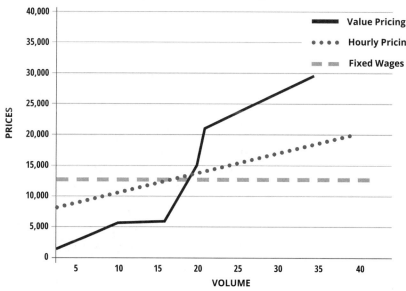

Figure 4.1 Leverage of Value Pricing

Barriers to Scaling a Tax Business

There are barriers beyond pricing that compromise your ability to leverage and scale your tax business.

Control Freak(-iness)

> ### *Dominique's Story*
>
> I am a recovering control freak. There, I said it! I truly believe I started my tax business, so I could exercise my control-freak desires. I didn't realize that when I started my business and worked hard to grow it, I actually designed my business with one of the most powerful detriments to my success in place: myself.
>
> I designed my practice to heavily rely on me. And while it might have been necessary when I first launched my business, it became a major weakness. I worked myself to the bone doing everything on my own. I even had clients I didn't really like, but I couldn't get rid of them because I couldn't afford to, and I was scared of a negative impact from firing clients.
>
> I was puzzled. I was helping some business owners that appeared to move from one successful company to the next, seemingly possessing a "golden touch." It's like the football coach who keeps winning everywhere he goes: he wins not because of the team he has at each organization, but because he has a winning system.
>
> At first, I thought it was because my business was different. I told myself, "It's special. It really needs my full attention and continuous review." What I didn't realize was that by asserting the uniqueness of my business I really locked myself into every detail of that business. And at some point I realized that it was too complicated to wean my business off its reliance on me. The belief in my importance was one of the most expensive and limiting beliefs that I could ever possess—and

at that time I owned that belief. That thought process literally cost me millions of dollars in lost growth—and don't even get me started on what it cost me personally.

Why did I have this false idea for so long? Because I equated the reduction in my company's reliance on me with a loss of control. The irony of this is that the more in control I thought I was, the less I actually was in control. The bottom line is I didn't own the business—the business owned me!

I came to a point where I needed a change. I started to wonder that if I didn't control my time and what I did with it, was I really experiencing the freedom that a business owner is supposed to enjoy? Was I really free when, if something happened to me, my family would get virtually nothing if they sold my business?

Lesson Learned: The more controlling I was in my business, the more I had to be there to take care of things, and the less freedom I really had.

If you find yourself reluctant to let go of tasks, your desire for control could cost you the ability to scale your business. Aside from facing time constraints, we are all limited physically when it comes to the amount of work we can complete. As long as your need to tend to all business functions consumes you, you are less likely to be able to grow your business—and more likely to live in a state of perpetual exhaustion.

Growing a service-based business requires labor support; you can't possibly do it all while multiplying the size of your company. You must hire well and be willing to trust those you have hired to carry out their responsibilities. Establishing excellent internal controls can ensure that you meet the level of quality you demand, while giving you tools to monitor the excellence of your services.

The irony of control is that you never really have it to begin with. Those who seek control have the tendency to overestimate their ability to control events. In reality, you can never fully control the outcome of anything. As your efforts to control the desired outcomes increase, more things are likely to go wrong, decreasing your chances to reach your goals.

Instead of relying on your ability to control the business, you need to rely on systems, your team, and the internal controls you create to achieve your desired results.

SALY Syndrome

Do you remember learning about SALY (Same As Last Year) in accounting classes? I clearly remember using this little shortcut to reduce my workload and apply the same analysis or procedures simply because we "did it that way last year."

Yet another symptom of overworking, the SALY syndrome runs rampant in the tax industry as tax professionals try to just get through their to-do list and get paid.

The risk in always relying on the SALY method is that you can never experience growth without changing the way things are done. Personally, I believe this is why the tax industry is broken. Practitioners long ago established protocols that everyone has been following since the first income tax was collected in 1913.

The funny thing about doing things "Same As Last Year" is that you can almost predict the future of your business. Want to know what your business will be doing a year from now? As long as nothing changes, you pretty much already know what to expect in revenues, workload, challenges, and outcomes. If you really want your business to change, you must change the way you do business!

Copying undesirable systems, pricing, staffing, and models either from your past experiences or those of others won't allow you to leverage or scale your business. If you want different results, you must do something differently to achieve them.

People Pleasing

I've met an awful lot of people pleasers in this industry. Perhaps on some level you started in the tax business because, like me, you love to solve problems. I can't think of a bigger problem than the feeling of having someone not like you. Perhaps it is the fear of disappointing someone or not being liked that leaves you so eager to please that you find it difficult to charge what you're worth.

As you can see from this chapter, your ability to scale your tax business depends on your ability to charge premium fees that are not attached to the amount of time your work takes you to complete. Further, you must actually charge for the work you do!

Have you ever "eaten time" because you didn't want to deal with possible push-back from your clients? Perhaps you've sometimes realized you've gone over your budgeted time but not wanted to approach the client to inform them of a higher charge. I've always hated billing my clients for short telephone calls and emails to answer questions (see Chapter 3 on attorney fees), and as a result, I never got paid for these things before I bundled my services. I wanted to please everyone, and therefore my ability to generate revenue suffered.

This need to please people can really materialize as you enter a new phase in your development by value-pricing. If you can take that leap of faith and face your fears, you will enjoy the rewards of being able to scale your business and experience greater freedom.

Giving It Away

As a teenager, I once had a very awkward conversation with my mother about "giving it away." I remember something about "why take care of the cow when you can get the milk for free" coming into the discussion. (I couldn't see, at the time, how that was remotely relevant for my request to attend a school dance, but that is a topic for a different book!)

As I progressed in my business ownership, I came to understand the meaning of this analogy. Whether grounded in my desire to please people or in my fear of rejection, I gave away nearly seven figures of income over the years in work I did for free. I think this habit of mine grew worse as my relationships with my clients deepened. It wasn't long before all of my customers were friends, and how could I charge substantial fees to friends?

If this is sounding all too familiar, you are not alone. Each year, I meet thousands of tax business owners, and one thing we all have in common is that at one time or another we have given away our expertise without charging for it.

The biggest problem with this is that you start conditioning people and building expectations of how to do business with you. Once you establish a precedent for how you charge for your worth, people expect it to continue, and it can be uncomfortable to break that habit.

How much do you believe you've given away over the years? Is it too painful to contemplate? One graduate recently shared he had given away several million dollars of tax-planning services during his 20-year career. Such realization is no doubt painful.

To solve this problem, consider the analogy of giving away inventory. If you owned a retail store, would you give away your merchandise? Of course not. You would not do so because there is an outside value assigned to your inventory, whereas it is difficult to see the value in an intangible product. Your expertise is your inventory, and this book demonstrates the value of it. You must carefully protect this asset, or you will never be able to create the kind of income you need to scale your business and leverage your services.

Showing the Value in Other Tax Services and Premium-Fee Billing for Compliance Work

By now, you are probably asking yourself, "I see the value in tax-planning services where you can calculate and show your value in dollars and cents, but how do I show the value of other tax services?" This is a valid concern. Let's say you develop a tax plan that creates $20,000 per year in tax savings; it is easy enough to show the benefit of a $5,000 planning fee. However, when it's time to prepare the tax returns, answer notices, reconcile accounting records, answer all those "quick questions," and do all the other work required by our clients, how can you quantify the value of these services?

I've found that packaging products and services together with definable added-value services makes showing the value easier. I use packages to offer all my services to clients. This way, I can apply the value from the tax-planning service to the group of services and establish my prices independent of how long the project takes to complete. For example, building a package of services including the tax plan, the tax returns, several phone calls and email consultations a year, accounting reconciliation, and notice responses allows you to position your services worth $20,000 per year for a fee of $12,000. In this scenario, you've now created a premium fee, highlighted your value to the individual, and shown the client that, based on the resulting tax savings, your services pay for themselves.

Creating Year-Round Cash Flow to Finance the Growth of Your Business

Another problem we face in the tax industry is the seasonal nature of our cash flow. Since typically the clients maintain control over the timing of the work (they approach you on their own terms when they are ready), it leaves the cash flow of the tax business unpredictable.

A solution to this is to create year-round monthly retainer agreements. If you bundle your services, it is easy to convert the costs into monthly agreements by simply turning the annual totals into monthly payments. Thereby you streamline your cash flow and receive income that is not connected to service hours.

Consider the ability to receive income while you are on vacation, holidays, and weekends—this is possible with a monthly retainer agreement. Another benefit of consistent year-round cash flow is that it makes it easier to plan resources needed to fulfill your promises to customers. Think about how much easier it would be to hire support knowing you have reliable cash flow to cover the overhead costs.

Consistent cash flow is a key to the scalability of any business. Without predictable, consistent, and regular cash flow, you never know if you can afford the resources you need to grow. Value-based pricing not only guarantees that you will get paid what you're worth now, but also that you can effectively scale your business and grow your worth in the future.

CHAPTER 5

Value-Pricing Your Services

By now, you may be asking yourself: How do I decide what price I should be charging? The first step in answering this question is to make sure you actually create value. Many professionals subconsciously fear the use of value-pricing. On some level, the ambiguity of the value of services traditionally offered by accountants creates confusion over how consumers view and value their work.

Examining the public's perception of the value of your work, you will notice that there is very little value attributed to tax compliance work. While some may value the security of complying with the law or the support you lend during an audit, it's difficult to translate this feeling to a quantifiable value. As I've mentioned before, the easiest way to quantify your value is to create monetary worth to the work you are doing. Tax planning offers this opportunity.

The first step in planning requires changing the way you work from a reactive approach to a proactive approach. Traditional tax work is reactive in nature. When you prepare a tax return, you are acting as a historian, recording what has already happened. There are very few opportunities to reduce tax once the year is over. As a result, there are very few things you can do to create quantifiable value for your customers when you are working reactively.

When you are able to work proactively, you plan for future transactions and take advantage of altering the circumstances of your clients' ways of doing business. This opens up the opportunity to take advantage of the resulting tax breaks later on. Proactive planning requires advance preparation, forethought, and clear communication from your clients about upcoming events.

It might seem impossible to change the way you work—it isn't an easy undertaking. Moving from a reactive approach to a proactive approach requires time and careful planning. This is primarily because both approaches are cyclical. Let's examine how each cycle works, and how you can create a plan to change your approach.

Reactive Cycle

The reactive cycle begins by allowing your clients to initiate the engagement. It starts with a client request for work, which you respond to. This is a key indicator that you are working reactively. If you wonder whether you are working reactively, ask yourself, "How do most of my projects begin?" If most of your work begins with the client request, you most likely work reactively.

Once the work comes in, it sets off a sequence of events that feed the reactive cycle. As new work arrives, the practitioner must enter it into the existing schedule. Priorities for the work are dictated by the procedures you use in your business. Some firms prioritize based on the importance or profitability of the client, for example. Once the work is entered into the workflow, the firm's workload increases, which in turn increases demand on business resources. As demand increases, there are reductions in available resources such as manpower and other support. As such, standards drop, and procedures can be missed. This creates additional pressure on the system, and less time is available to seek additional work. Since new business is not sought proactively, new work begins when a customer requests it, and the cycle continues. (See Figure 5.1.)

Figure 5.1 Reactive Cycle

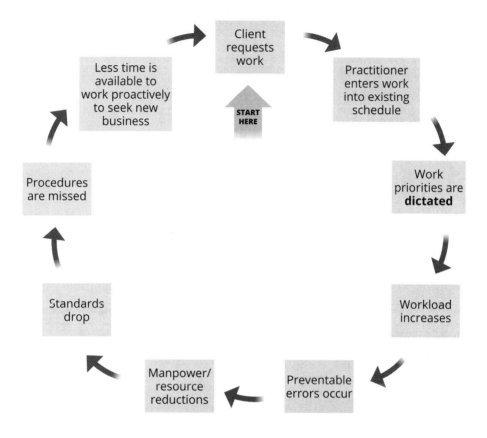

Many negative working conditions originate from following the reactive approach. Consider the reason tax pros work long hours. In the traditional billing model, tax business owners are paid at the end of the engagement. This billing method transfers control of your cash flow to your client. Since your pay depends on delivery of the work, you furiously work late hours, weekends, and holidays, so you can deliver the product and collect the revenues.

Key Indicators You Are Working Reactively

Your primary work consists of the following:

- Recording history
- Reconciling records
- Documenting transactions that have already happened
- Responding to client requests
- Taking action because something else requires it

Proactive Cycle

The proactive cycle begins with prescheduled work. With a proactive approach, you plan how you will meet your clients' needs. Your plan is based upon what is best for the client and for your business. This provides the opportunity to prioritize the work and plan resources year-round. When using a monthly maintenance agreement, your routine consultations are prescheduled, and you meet with people according to your plan. During these sessions, you are optimizing the plan and ascertaining the work needed to accomplish it. Since you are working according to schedule, you use your planned resources and follow your procedures to complete the work. The procedures include internal controls that prevent errors and maintain your standards. As work is being completed, you follow your schedule and proactively seek new business, which continues the cycle. (See Figure 5.2.)

Key Indicators You Are Working Proactively

Your primary work consists of the following:

- Pre-scheduling consultations
- Planning for future transactions
- Projecting scenarios
- Structuring events that are currently taking place
- Prescheduling meetings with clients

Figure 5.2 Proactive Cycle

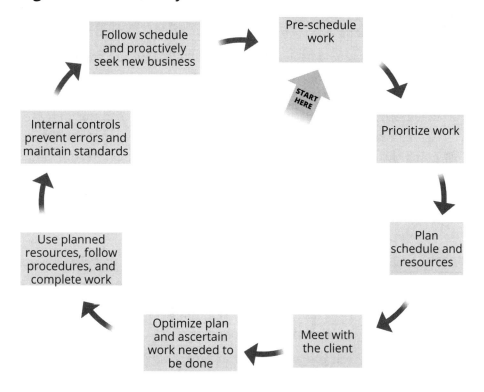

- Planning firm resources according to your prescheduled work plan
- Prescheduled business growth activities

Getting Derailed

There's a fine line between both the reactive and proactive cycles, which makes it easy to become derailed. Be careful of incidents that can derail your work approach; you may fall off the proactive cycle and return to a reactive approach.

These incidents include loss of key staff or resources, working on engagements not included in your plan or schedule, losing a revenue source or referral partner, technical issues, not having access to the right tools, and personal issues such as relationship difficulties, health issues, and family demands.

Once you become derailed and find yourself working reactively, it's imperative to have a plan you can follow to get back on track. I recommend having what I call a "recovery card," which includes steps you can take to return to proactive planning. For example, you may remind yourself to read your plan and select one task to perform; sometimes, just going through the motions of working proactively can restore your intentions to work optimally. Another suggestion is to immediately fill your open work schedule. Once you recover your momentum, you can reestablish your proactive approach and seek new business.

Suggested Steps to Return to the Proactively Cycle:

- Make an advance plan for how to return to the proactive cycle
- Read your weekly action list and complete one task from the list
- Fill your open schedule and follow it
- Stop the work you are doing and proactively seek new business

Other Benefits of Working Proactively

Working proactively helps mitigate some of the pitfalls of running a tax business. For example, when you preschedule work, you have the benefit of planning the resources you'll need. You are able to allocate enough time to allow your team to follow established procedures and use your internal quality controls. Working proactively also allows you to more accurately project cash flow and income, so you can adequately secure the necessary resources. A proactive approach builds confidence in your ability to generate, sustain, and grow income. When you pre-schedule your work and get paid in advance, there is no need to work long hours as in a traditionally run tax business. Your income is predictable and higher, and it allows you to plan time off for other interests, vacations, and family commitments. In short, a proactive work model allows you to have a life outside of work. And your life is more likely to look like the one you dreamed of having when you decided to start your business.

Establishing Your Price

To your customer, the important factor in determining how much they are willing to pay for a service is ultimately what they consider to be the perceived value of your service. That is where pricing becomes more of an art. With this in mind, the most important part of pricing is to focus on the value you can deliver and ensure that you clearly communicate that value to the prospective customer. In all purchasing decisions, the customer must believe that it is a better deal to give their money to you rather than to keep it and do nothing, or to give it to your competitor.

Since it has already been established that hourly billing can limit the profitability of your business, the next question to answer is: What portion of the value created is an appropriate price?

Since we aren't always aware what our prospective customer considers valuable before our initial discussion, I prefer to attend the pricing meeting with three prices in mind. To prepare, I establish a minimum price, a fair price, and a GTGM (Good for Them, Good for Me) price. As the meeting progresses and I am better able to determine how much value I can create for the customer, I select one of the prices I've brought to the meeting.

Consider this five-step process when setting your minimum price:

1. **Determine your annual income requirements.** What is the cost of maintaining your desired lifestyle? Establishing this cost as your minimum take-home pay is a good starting point for creating your pricing structure. Beginning with how much you'd like to earn is a logical first step in taking control of your revenue.

2. **Compute overhead.** What costs support your work style? What resources do you need to create your desired work environment? Including this cost in your fee structure ensures that you'll make enough money to build a business that sustains your preferred workload.

3. **Choose a profit margin.** Select an attractive profit margin that will add value to your business. Most tax businesses are valued by using a multiplier against annual gross revenue. One of the factors that affect this multiplier is the profit margin. Industry averages for tax firms reveal average profit margins of approximately 40 percent. To increase the attractiveness of your margin, select one that is higher than industry averages.

4. **Calculate your company's capacity for engagements.** How much work can your business comfortably complete while maintaining adequate focus on delivering ultimate value? This becomes easier to calculate if you have been tracking costs per project. For example, if I know my preparer's salary, benefits, and taxes cover her ability to manage six specific client relationships throughout the year, I can determine that she has the capacity for these specific projects. If this information is not available, you may need to start by creating a projection of your current workload and the amount of resources required for your current commitments. I recommend assigning projects to individual staff or as staff teams. In this regard, you can determine the capacity for your current staffing resources for the number of engagements they can accommodate given your required value-creation goals. Once you have identified this capacity, multiply it by 80 percent. Do this for each type of project you offer.

5. **Finally, total items 1 to 3 and divide by item 4.** This becomes your minimum price, or price floor for each project.

The next two prices to consider are more subjective to determine. In short, you must determine at what point the customer considers your price a better deal for them to pay you for the work you propose in lieu of taking no action or working with your competitor.

Questions to consider when setting a "fair price"

Since it is illegal to create your tax-planning fee as a derivative of the savings, I like to project a customer's answers to the following questions as a way to develop a "fair price."

1. At what price would the customer consider your engagement a good deal?
2. At what price would the customer consider your engagement too expensive to be a good deal?
3. What are the current returns on investment?
4. What will it cost the customer if they use your competitor or fail to take action?
5. What has it cost the customer over the last five years in missed opportunities?
6. At what price would your customer consider your engagement so low that they don't believe the value you project?

Questions to consider when setting your "Good for Them, Good for Me" (GTGM) price:

1. At what price would the customer believe you are more interested in your income than in doing what is best for them?
2. What price would be your "brag" price—a price that you'd want to brag about to your friends?
3. What is the projected value over the next five years?
4. What price provides more freedom for you than your average prices?
5. What other income do you predict generating as a result of doing business with this customer?

Preparing to Quote a Price

There are three steps when preparing yourself to quote your price. You may be surprised to learn that out of the three essentials, none of them have anything to do with your business or your services! All three essentials to preparing to quote a price are focused on the client: what they find valuable, and how to build their trust and confidence in you.

The first step in the process is taking the client's perspective. It's important to understand what they believe they are looking for and need in the relationship. You can identify this by asking questions. When implementing this step with existing clients, call them in for a mid-year interview and really touch base with what they find valuable about the services you already provide, what obstacles they face in their business, and what dreams they have for the future.

Listening carefully as your client shares their perspective with you will help you identify what they find valuable now or may find valuable as you build your specific offering. The benefit of truly understanding what your client finds valuable is that you can offer it in your range of services. Be sure to take your client's point of view on specific results they expect to achieve if they were to discover a solution to their problems or a shortcut to their dreams.

The second step is to clarify their results. Restate to your client what you've heard them share and the specific results they would experience if you were to solve their problem or help them accomplish their goals. If they are having difficulty articulating a specific result, attempt to help them clarify by suggesting common results you've seen in other businesses.

Finally, the third step is to build trust and confidence. This is not something that occurs in one interaction with the customer, but is a process you create over time. Being specific about timelines and expectations, making sure to keep your delivery promises and appointments on time, and only offering services you are prepared to and capable of fulfilling are all actions that lead to building trust and confidence in you as an advisor.

When determining your price for an individual customer, select a price that is somewhere between your minimum price as calculated above and a point where it still makes financial sense for the customer to proceed with the work given the specific value of the results you'll help create.

In order for someone to change their current solution, the perceived cost of changing has to be low while the cost of not taking action has to be high. Introducing higher fees based on value might appear to be a high cost of taking action at first glance, but it may be small when compared to the high cost of not taking action. You want to be able to convey that the loss of the value you can create with your expertise is drastically higher than the cost of investing with you to take action. For example, if I can save someone $25,000 per year in tax savings, and my price, while higher than hourly billing, is just $10,000, the customer would have to be willing to walk away from a net gain of $15,000 to not accept the offer. In other words, your price has to make financial sense before someone will accept your offer.

In some cases, depending on what you learn when you clarify their responses, some customers may be willing to take action even if the cost is high when compared to the cost of not taking action. For example, when learning about my client's gain, if I realize they are seeking value in the form of business coaching as their business grows over the next three years, I may be able to charge $20,000 for my services even though it would result in a smaller tangible net gain for the customer. The fact that what the customer finds valuable is something that I can offer represents more than just financial value in the equation. I may also help them clarify their gain in terms of future revenue growth resulting from the coaching, so, as I present my price, I can reference that gain in the discussion.

Raising Prices

I'm frequently asked about price increases—when and how to raise prices. My suggestions depend on how you are billing for your services.

If you use bundled service agreements (see chapter 4), you can raise your prices each year for each agreement or when circumstances and offerings change.

If you charge separately for each service, analyze your most popular services. When you bill separately, you run a risk in raising prices across the board. You may see a decline in some of your less popular product offerings when you raise prices. Instead, identify your most popular services and raise prices on those services first. You may be surprised when people fail to notice the increase! For less popular services, consumers are more sensitive to pricing, and they may end up declining a service they've purchased in the past.

This logic can also assist you in deciding which services to include in a bundled service agreement. Combining less popular services with more popular ones helps you get paid for work that your customers may not normally request. I also use this strategy for services I typically don't charge for. For example, if I am reluctant to bill for things like "quick" telephone consults or notice responses, I make sure to include them in my bundled service agreements. This guarantees I'll get paid for the service without having to bill separately for the work.

Whichever method you choose, be sure to routinely increase your prices. Smaller, regular price increases are more successful than infrequent, large increases.

Alexander's Story

Alexander used to love his tax business but just felt burnt out. After 25 years in business, he felt like he had built himself a job. And it was actually even worse than a job—it was a job where he had to not only do all the work, but also carry all the overhead, stress, and responsibilities.

If you've been in the tax industry for a while, I'm sure you know exactly what this CPA means. The real challenge Alexander faced wasn't that his tax business wasn't a good business—it had supported him and his family comfortably for years. It was just that he had maxed out what he knew about how to build a service business.

He knew how to run the day-to-day "job," of building his business, but he didn't know how to grow and develop it as an investment. No one had ever taught him how to do that. Alexander routinely offered tax advice to his clients, but did not charge separately for the service. Worse, he noticed that people didn't seem to implement the recommendations that he put the extra time and thought into developing. During his first year in the CTC program, Alexander was able to shift his mindset from doing the day-to-day "job" of his business to building a middle-stage, manager-owned business. Alexander learned to create a better strategic plan to grow his business; how to build better systems, intelligently grow his team, and develop strong internal controls, so that he knew that things were getting done the right way and at the right time. For Alexander and his business, it was a breath of fresh air.

In the second year, Alexander developed a technique of offering tax planning to his current clients. Rather than creating a large tax plan each year, he selected one tax-reduction idea and requested meetings with each client. At the meeting, he presented the idea and said, "Here's what we're going to do, and here is the cost." Using this assumed closing technique helped Alexander sell 52 tax plans that year and his revenues increased by 40 percent. The additional benefit of Alexander's new way of offering tax-planning advice was that when he billed separately for this service, his clients actively implemented his ideas. Treating the tax plan as a separate engagement meant people would actually reduce their taxes while Alexander's income increased!

Part of these results came from better tactics—knowing exactly how to do the "what to do." Tactics are the concrete actions you need to perform in order to implement your strategy. Other reasons for these results came from having a support and accountability structure for the first time in his business; it made sure he was consistently doing the "how" and "what."

By the third year, Alexander went on to lead one of our mastermind groups where he worked with his own group of Certified Tax Coaches to share the tactics he used himself. Later that year, he was a finalist for our CTC of the Year Award.

The best part for Alexander is how much more enjoyable his business has become. It is vibrant and growing, and he's got a team utilizing internal systems and controls, so his business relies markedly less on him.

Lesson Learned: Notifying your clients of your prices for tax-planning services rather than asking permission guarantees increased revenues for you and reduced taxes for your customers.

CHAPTER 6

Selling Premium-Fee Tax Plans

Converting Clients from Tax Preparation to Tax Planning

Now that I've whetted your appetite for adding tax plans to your services, I would like to demonstrate how you can convert your transactional business based on tax return preparation to a tax-planning business. Shifting your focus in this way is critical if you want to get paid what you're worth. Before you think this is impossible, I ask you to play along and humor me. The common trend among successful business owners is the willingness to adapt. For this chapter, forget traditional tax business practices and hear me out.

We've already analyzed the idea that when you offer tax-planning services, you convert your business to a business that sells cash. This highlights the psychology behind why people make purchasing decisions and why people will pay more for something they want than for something they need.

When you offer tax planning to your clients and focus on the value and savings you can create for them, they want this service; you are practically offering them money, and they will be willing to pay more for such a service.

In contrast, when your primary offering is something people need, like preparing their income tax returns, it becomes difficult to see the value, and it isn't something they want; rather, it's a service they need. Accordingly, they are less willing to pay premium fees.

Consider similar examples in other industries. For instance, you want a sports car, but you need a station wagon—which one typically costs more? You need a health checkup, but you want plastic surgery. You need a place to live, but you want a house on the beach.

However, just because clients want what you offer, doesn't mean it's easy getting them to pay more than you've been charging in the past. You may encounter some objections to your new service as you begin to shift away from focusing on compliance work to focusing on proactive planning work. Trust me: once you demonstrate the benefit of proactive tax planning, your clients want it.

The easiest thing about approaching current clients with an opportunity to reduce their taxes is that you already have a relationship with them. They view you as a trusted advisor and take your advice on financial matters. Remember the three essentials you need to prepare to quote your price? In working with your existing clients, you've already built trust and confidence. Another advantage is that you already have all the information you need to create an optimal environment for offering your tax-planning service. That is, you have all the tax information required to create an estimate of the savings potential.

The first step in converting your existing clients to accept your tax-planning proposal is to analyze their current tax position. Review your files and look over their prior year tax returns. What opportunities for improvement do you see? If necessary, run some tax projections using your ideas for tax reductions and identify the savings potential. For each idea you develop, keep a running total of the tax savings. Finally, when you've developed several impactful ideas, it's time for a conversation with your customer.

The Secret Sauce for Selling Premium-Fee Tax Plans

Once you've identified the savings potential (at this point in the process, you have merely built a quick estimate—it should take only 30 to 60 minutes), it's time to communicate this to your client.

You might recall the importance of communicating the value of your services to your client. This becomes even more important when approaching someone you've already been working with. Now that you are offering something completely different, it becomes more important to demonstrate why they want what you are offering. Begin by letting them know you've been reviewing their information and tell them that you have some ideas that can save them money. Describe the tax-planning process and be sure to let them know the savings potential by accepting your offer to create the plan. Once you've described the process and the value of doing the plan, quote your fee as close as possible to the discussion of the plan's value. Using this technique positions your fee in context to the value you create rather than to some factor imagined by the client. (When left undefined, people will attribute your fees to what they know. If you've been billing hourly in the past, they will connect your fee to time.)

Dean's Story

Dean, an Enrolled Agent, became certified in tax planning in 2010. The second night of his certification training, Dean met some prospective clients in the hotel bar and began talking about the value of tax planning. When he entered class the next day, Dean shared his success in selling a $5,000 tax plan the night before, without even seeing the bar patron's tax returns!

Later, Dean developed his own technique for selling premium-fee tax-planning services to his current clients. Rather than convincing the clients of the value of the plan by showing the saving's amounts, Dean focused on the changing tax laws as his motivator. He selected prospective clients from his tax return database and called each one in for a meeting. Dean shared his concerns for the continuous tax uncertainty in Washington and as such let each person know he was taking a more serious approach to protecting them from increasing tax rates. In his first four months as a certified tax planner, Dean sold over $40,000 in new tax-planning engagements—all without mentioning a savings amount.

Lesson Learned: Find out what's important to your clients and present your tax-planning service as a solution to their problem. It will motivate them to purchase your service.

A great starting place for selecting clients to approach would be your tax-preparation software database. Many software applications allow you to filter your reports based on select criteria. I suggest using a tax-reduction strategy you are familiar with and run a database report to filter for clients most likely to qualify for it.

Let's say you are searching for sole proprietorships that may benefit from changing their entity: Build a report showing you tax returns with Schedule C filings. You can then do more analysis of these returns to further identify candidates. If, for example, you want to look for real estate tax strategies, you may run your filtered report selecting Schedule E filings. These reports serve as your initial list of prospective clients.

Dominique's Story

When I made the decision to begin charging premium fees for separate tax-planning engagements, I first turned to my existing clients to test my process and pricing and prove the product was viable. Boy, was I scared! I really feared how my clients might react, and worried I'd be rejected or scolded for offending someone.

> I was so terrified that I decided to initially select five of my favorite clients and offer to create plans for free to get their feedback.
>
> I approached the first two clients and had positive presentations. When I asked my long-time "friend-clients" how much they would pay for a similar service, they encouraged me to increase my fees and bring this to market. I was so encouraged by their responses that I decided I'd given away enough of my expertise inventory. I abandoned my original plan to offer five plans for free and instead sold plans to the remaining three people on my list.
>
> **Lesson Learned:** Working with people you trust and know can be an easy way to get the feedback you need to build confidence and launch a new product.

Tax-Planning Outlook

I'm frequently asked what the future demand will be for tax-planning services. People want to know if this is a lucrative offering that will be around in the future. My belief is that there has never been a better time to be in the business of tax planning. Deficits running out of control, restrictive congressional budgets, and increasing economic legislation are good indications that, if anything, tax-planning services will be more in demand. Taking a historical look at income taxes will help put this into perspective.

When Congress first imposed taxes, back in 1913, the top rate was only 7 percent. Can you imagine that? That top rate soared to 73 percent after World War I. In 1929, it dropped to 24 percent. It was 25 percent during the first two years of the Great Depression, and then it amounted to as high as 92 percent under the Eisenhower Administration. These fluctuations are not just a thing of the past. Since Eisenhower, there have been many changes: tax rates dropped to as low as 31 percent during George H.W. Bush's presidency; while Clinton was in office, it rose to 39 percent; between 2003 and 2012, it went back down to 35 percent.

As seen in Figure 6.1, President Bush actually took office with a budget surplus—that's if you accept the government's own accounting rules. But with the combination of lower taxes, higher spending, and a higher defense budget, it really pushed the deficit up to record levels.

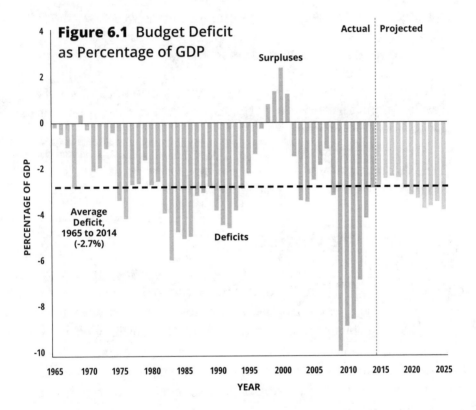

Figure 6.1 Budget Deficit as Percentage of GDP

In recent years, the Office of Management and Budget reported an annual deficit of $1.3 trillion—that's almost $4,000 for every man, woman, and child in this country. Our national debt has topped $14 trillion; that's $41,000 for each of us.

If recent history tells us anything, it's this: Be prepared for anything to happen, because it's going to happen fast. Who would have expected the Department of the Treasury to commit $30 billion to bail out Bear Stearns? And who would have expected it to spend just as much to bail out AIG in the wake of Hurricane Katrina? The Department of the

Treasury actually bought 80 percent of the company. Who would have guessed that the government would wind up committing up to $700 billion to buying stakes in banks!

The Washington Heritage Foundation, a conservative think tank, conducted a study estimating how high taxes would have to rise to completely eliminate the deficit. And it's what you'd think it is; the numbers get pretty ugly. Marginal rates would top out at 85 percent for top earners and 24 percent in place of our lowest bracket right now, which is 10 percent. Basically, income tax rates would need to more than double to cover the national deficit. The number would get even uglier if Washington does not raise taxes on families making under $250,000: the top rates would have to go all the way up to 142 percent, which, of course, is impossible. I have to say that not even the accounting geniuses who ran Enron can make numbers like that work.

Just know this: Higher taxes are coming—they simply can't be avoided, and they won't be confined to the rich. They're coming for everyone—even middle-class clients, who don't see a need for tax planning. People are aware of this; we don't have to educate them on this. People just figure that's what's going to happen. How does this relate to you? Your clients are afraid. The topic is constantly in the media. There are dozens of talking heads all over television and radio screaming about it. Most of your existing clients—and, not to forget, your potential clients—think about it. They know that huge deficits result in higher taxes.

If you are not offering relief, especially for your current clients, they're not getting the proper guidance they want. Think about it again in terms of selling people something they need versus something they want: simply the assumption that tax rates will go up gives you the opportunity to offer your clients something they want. In this case, they want relief from the higher taxes that are coming their way.

Another factor working in your favor is the economy. Business owners are really struggling, and they need more cash. They don't want to lay people off or pull their business back, but they often have no other choice. You can offer them something they want: cash in their pockets. Because they're not paying it to the IRS, they will spend the money. They buy because it is what they want right now. If you think they don't have the money to afford this service, the reality is they can either pay it to you, or they can pay it to the IRS. The difference is that when you can offer a struggling business increased cash flow, you're giving them something that they want.

I've spent a significant amount of time talking about our history of taxes. I hope you see the volatility of our tax system combined with a struggling economy as the "perfect storm" for tax planning. Right now, you've got the ideal opportunity to become a leader in your field and offer clients something that they want in the process, while you get paid what you're worth.

Frequently Asked Questions

1. **Do you use engagement letters for planning engagements?**

    Absolutely. Engagement letters are extremely valuable for several reasons. I benefit from using them because they clearly define the scope of the engagement. It's as simple as altering your existing letter to talk about a tax plan instead of a tax return engagement. Engagement letters for tax planning clearly identify what's going to happen during that engagement, so there's no confusion, and everyone is on the same page.

2. **When you present the final tax plan to the client, what documents and/or software do you use?**

    Certified Tax Planners use special software that presents a written report in easy-to-understand terms. The report is full of the details of the tax plan we create. We also use Excel spreadsheets, Word documents, etc. It's important to customize the information for your client. Keep it simple and back up your work with references and footnotes to tax codes and court rulings. All of this is provided for CTC members.

3. **What type of client is a primary candidate for tax planning?**

   Although almost all of your clients are viable candidates for tax planning, small-business owners, large-business owners, investors, and real estate investors provide opportunities. I recommend measuring your options with every client to determine whether or not to suggest offering them tax planning.

Complimentary Pricing Essentials Tool Kit

Includes:

Worksheets from this book

Price Increase Announcement Template

Price Increase Package Opt-In Certificate Template

Price Offer Opt-Out Certificate Template

Audit Protection Package Profit Analyzer

Get Paid What You're Worth Home Video Course

Just visit www.GetPaidForYourWorth.com

CHAPTER 7

Using a Tax Rescue to Sell Planning Services

By now, you're aware that clients do not really want to file their tax returns (yet, they need to), and that it's important to identify what they actually want: to keep as much of their money as possible. People want to pay less in tax. People want cash. Based on knowing this, the best way to bring value to your tax relationships is through tax planning. When you focus on tax planning, you can value-price your services and get paid what you're worth.

I like to think of the value we bring to taxpayers as "tax rescue." The concept is simple: as tax planners, we rescue people from the mistake of paying too much in tax.

How to Use a Tax Return to Sell Planning Services

We've previously looked at the elements of tax planning, and how you can convert clients from tax preparation to tax planning. But how can you effectively use a tax return to sell planning services? There is a secret formula for this: the four steps below are the key to helping you change the way you bill and get paid what you're worth. If you take the following steps to sell tax-planning services, you can use the power of a tax return to easily demonstrate your value to the taxpayer and leave them eager to hire you at premium fees to "rescue" them.

1. **Revisit Tax Returns from the Past**

   The first thing that you want to do is scan past tax returns for mistakes and missed opportunities. This is super easy to do for existing clients because you have the tax returns and other important information right at your fingertips. When working with a prospective client, ask them to provide their most recent tax returns. A simple strategy for ensuring they provide what you need is to ask them to do this as a condition for the initial meeting. When a prospect calls you after being referred, having seen your ad, or having found your website, you usually set up a meeting—be sure to ask them to bring their tax returns, so you can look for mistakes and missed opportunities.

2. **Scan the Tax Returns for Mistakes and Missed Opportunities**

   Next, look through the tax returns for indicators of potential savings. I recommend you review each tax return in a systematic way, so you can improve your accuracy and speed with which you accomplish this step each time. When you become certified in tax planning, you will gain a rich knowledge base of ideas, tactics, and indicators, so that you know which areas to focus on.

   With each idea you find, quantify how much it is worth in the form of tax reductions to the taxpayer, and keep a running total as you go along.

3. **Communicate What You Find**

   Many techniques and methods can help you improve your sales conversion rates as you communicate your findings to your prospective clients. While I am not able to summarize all of those ideas here, the important thing to remember is the significance of demonstrating your value. This discussion is your opportunity to provide some value to the taxpayer (by explaining your findings), as well as to convey to them the value of the work you're offering.

I prefer to give a brief overview of what I've noticed in their tax history and ask questions about entity choice, business operations, and expected changes in the future. Next, I detail the amounts of the tax reduction they will realize by moving forward with a full tax strategy.

4. **Quoting Your Fee in the "Safe Zone"**

    Providing the tax savings amount not only satisfies them, but it helps to build trust and confidence. It is also a great opportunity to inform your clients of your fees in the shelter of the "safe zone" of the savings that you will be creating for them.

Again, the idea is that the more you connect your fees to the value you create, the more you detach the idea of your value being the time that you spend on the engagement. It's also important to be able to establish the value you create as a return on their investment.

I am not suggesting in any way that your fee is based on these savings, or that you are charging a percentage of the savings or anything of that nature. In fact, Circular 230 prohibits us from doing that. If you present the fee in the same space as the tax savings, you enable yourself to give context to the financial impact of the transaction. In turn, you'll be able to sell your tax-planning services at higher fees, and the client will be excited to pay your fees because now you are giving them what they want instead of what they need—which is one of the keys to getting paid what you're worth.

Practice Selling Planning Services

Now that you know how to use a tax return to sell planning services, it's essential to practice doing it. Figure 7.1 provides a narrative to help you practice.

82 Get Paid What You're Worth

Figure 7.1 Brooks Family Tax Return

Form **1040**	Department of the Treasury—Internal Revenue Service **U.S. Individual Income Tax Return** **2015**	(99)	IRS Use Only—Do not write or staple in this space.

For the year Jan. 1–Dec. 31, 2009, or other tax year beginning , 2009, ending , 20 | OMB No. 1545-0074

Label (See instructions on page 14.) Use the IRS label. Otherwise, please print or type.

Your first name and initial: Howard
Last name: Brooks
Your social security number: 1 2 3 4 5 6 7

If a joint return, spouse's first name and initial: Virginia
Last name: Brooks
Spouse's social security number: 1 2 3 4 5 6 7

Home address (number and street). If you have a P.O. box, see page 14. Apt. no.
620 Eighth Avenue
▲ You must enter your SSN(s) above. ▲

City, town or post office, state, and ZIP code. If you have a foreign address, see page 14.
New York, NY 10018

Checking a box below will not change your tax or refund.

Presidential Election Campaign ▶ Check here if you, or your spouse if filing jointly, want $3 to go to this fund (see page 14) ▶ ☐ You ☐ Spouse

Filing Status
Check only one box.

1 ☐ Single
2 ☑ Married filing jointly (even if only one had income)
3 ☐ Married filing separately. Enter spouse's SSN above and full name here. ▶
4 ☐ Head of household (with qualifying person). (See page 15.) If the qualifying person is a child but not your dependent, enter this child's name here. ▶
5 ☐ Qualifying widow(er) with dependent child (see page 16)

Exemptions

6a ☑ **Yourself.** If someone can claim you as a dependent, **do not** check box 6a .
b ☑ Spouse
c Dependents:
(1) First name Last name
(2) Dependent's social security number
(3) Dependent's relationship to you
(4) ✓ if qualifying child for child tax credit (see page 17)

Boxes checked on 6a and 6b: **2**
No. of children on 6c who:
• lived with you
• did not live with you due to divorce or separation (see page 18)
Dependents on 6c not entered above

If more than four dependents, see page 17 and check here ▶ ☐

d Total number of exemptions claimed .
Add numbers on lines above ▶ **2**

Income

Attach Form(s) W-2 here. Also attach Forms W-2G and 1099-R if tax was withheld.

If you did not get a W-2, see page 22.

Enclose, but do not attach, any payment. Also, please use Form 1040-V.

7 Wages, salaries, tips, etc. Attach Form(s) W-2 . | 7 |
8a Taxable interest. Attach Schedule B if required . | 8a | 27
b Tax-exempt interest. **Do not** include on line 8a . | 8b |
9a Ordinary dividends. Attach Schedule B if required . | 9a |
b Qualified dividends (see page 22) . | 9b |
10 Taxable refunds, credits, or offsets of state and local income taxes (see page 23) . | 10 |
11 Alimony received . | 11 |
12 Business income or (loss). Attach Schedule C or C-EZ . | 12 | 78,385
13 Capital gain or (loss). Attach Schedule D if required. If not required, check here ▶ ☐ | 13 |
14 Other gains or (losses). Attach Form 4797 . | 14 |
15a IRA distributions . 15a | b Taxable amount (see page 24) | 15b |
16a Pensions and annuities 16a | b Taxable amount (see page 25) | 16b |
17 Rental real estate, royalties, partnerships, S corporations, trusts, etc. Attach Schedule E | 17 |
18 Farm income or (loss). Attach Schedule F . | 18 |
19 Unemployment compensation in excess of $2,400 per recipient (see page 27) . | 19 |
20a Social security benefits 20a 19,024 | b Taxable amount (see page 27) | 20b | 16,170
21 Other income. List type and amount (see page 29) | 21 |
22 Add the amounts in the far right column for lines 7 through 21. This is your **total income** ▶ | 22 | 94,582

Adjusted Gross Income

23 Educator expenses (see page 29) . | 23 |
24 Certain business expenses of reservists, performing artists, and fee-basis government officials. Attach Form 2106 or 2106-EZ | 24 |
25 Health savings account deduction. Attach Form 8889 . | 25 |
26 Moving expenses. Attach Form 3903 . | 26 |
27 One-half of self-employment tax. Attach Schedule SE . | 27 | 5,538
28 Self-employed SEP, SIMPLE, and qualified plans . | 28 |
29 Self-employed health insurance deduction (see page 30) | 29 | 9,214
30 Penalty on early withdrawal of savings . | 30 |
31a Alimony paid b Recipient's SSN ▶ | 31a | 5,000
32 IRA deduction (see page 31) . | 32 |
33 Student loan interest deduction (see page 34) . | 33 |
34 Tuition and fees deduction. Attach Form 8917 . | 34 |
35 Domestic production activities deduction. Attach Form 8903 | 35 |
36 Add lines 23 through 31a and 32 through 35 . | 36 | 19,752.
37 Subtract line 36 from line 22. This is your **adjusted gross income** ▶ | 37 | 74,830

For Disclosure, Privacy Act, and Paperwork Reduction Act Notice, see page 97. Cat. No. 11320B Form **1040** (2015)

Figure 7.1 shows a past tax return for the Brooks family. The Brooks family is on extension for the current year, and they have brought their prior year tax return to your initial client meeting.

This is a real case that I worked on in my practice. You will notice that the numbers are not outrageous, but I created tax savings for the client based on this information. The numbers are factual, but, of course, the identities have been changed to protect the clients' privacy.

First, let's review the background of the Brooks family. Howard and Virginia Brooks own a software sales and support business called Brooks Data. During your initial meeting with the Brookses, they indicate that they have been feeling the tax pinch for quite some time. Howard Brooks is the taxpayer, and he is approaching retirement age. Over the last 10 years, he has been training their son, William, to someday take over the business. William is currently on payroll, and he pays for his own medical insurance through a single policy for his family.

William's current accountant told him that he doesn't have enough expenses to take a deduction for his medical expenses. William spends about $6,750 per year in medical insurance premiums. What the accountant probably means is that William doesn't have more than 10 percent of his AGI in medical expenses in order to fully deduct that expense on his Schedule A.

Virginia Brooks was recently laid off from her job, prompting her to start doing the bookkeeping for the family business. She also pays herself wages through the business to replace her salary from her previous job.

Let's say the Brooks family was referred to you by Virginia's personal trainer, who is also a current client of yours. They have heard great things about you, so they're really eager to see what you can do for them. They also know your focus is on tax planning, and they want to know if there is anything that you can do to improve their current situation.

Note that many tax plans that you will sell in your practice will not initially come in as tax plans. Clients usually do not come in saying, "I want a tax plan," but they may mention something in conversation that you can recognize as an indicator that they are in need of a tax plan. In the case of the Brooks family, they may say something more to the tune of, "I want to figure out a way to bring my son into the business." As the tax expert, it's up to you to identify other requests as tax-planning opportunities. And because there are tax consequences, the tax plan deserves the time and attention that it needs—and therefore it requires premium fees. So get paid what you're worth for it!

Following the formula, start by scanning the Brooks family's past tax return for mistakes and missed opportunities to create some savings. Use the information from the narrative and Figure 7.1 to estimate how much they can save in annual taxes. Also, take this time to identify any future tax opportunities that you don't see in the past tax returns.

As you are looking through the tax returns, make note of your ideas for tax opportunities based on the narrative. You can do this on something similar to a "tax savings worksheet," which is shown in Figure 7.2 below.

Figure 7.2 Tax Savings Worksheet

TAX STRATEGIES	TAX SAVINGS CREATED
IDEA 1:	$
IDEA 2:	$
IDEA 3:	$
IDEA 4:	$
TOTAL POTENTIAL SAVINGS	$

In your notes, begin by writing down what you know based on the information given in the narrative and based on what you see in the tax return, including the following:

- The Brookses run a software sales and support business.
- They own the business as a Schedule C sole proprietorship.

It's important to remember that the tax return will not tell you everything you need to know to create your early estimates. The initial client interview is extremely valuable when selling planning services. You'll need to rely on your listening skills to identify pathways to opportunities. And you must listen for other clues that the tax return doesn't give you as to what kinds of savings you can create for the client. Information you may acquire from the initial interview includes:

- Howard Brooks wishes to retire at some point in the near future.
- Although currently an employee, William Brooks is going to take over the family business when his father retires.

Now, let's get into identifying potential tax savings. I highly recommend that you develop a good technique for reviewing tax returns. I use a systematic approach to this; it's a technique that you can repeat each and every time you review a tax return. Additionally, use your own practice aids to help you with this, whether it is a checklist, a procedure, or a flowchart of how you look at a tax return. Practice aids allow you to do two things:

- To perform quick reviews
- To avoid missing any tax-planning opportunities

If you don't have a good technique for reviewing tax returns, create one. Use one technique consistently, so that you can get faster and more accurate results.

Referring to Figure 7.2, use the tax savings worksheet to take notes and begin generating ideas for the Brooks family.

Begin with the front of the tax return and identify how the Brooks family members are earning their incomes, and recognize other items of relevance. You might notice the following areas:

- Entity selection
- Medical expenses and how they are being deducted currently
- Retirement contributions

Examining how the Brookses have chosen to organize their business is a good starting point to identify savings opportunities.

You can see from the tax returns that the Brookses report their business as a Schedule C sole proprietorship and net $78,000 each year. Consider an S Corporation as an alternative. Having an S Corporation might provide an opportunity to save the Brookses self-employment tax. We know that the Brooks family is in the business of software sales and support. Thus, there's even a possibility of using more than one business to handle the different functions in the core business. Perhaps using an S Corporation will enable you to split the earnings between a reasonable wage and distributions to create some savings in self-employment tax. On your first line on the tax savings worksheet, you can fill in, "Form an S Corporation." The tax savings created from that change could represent anywhere from $4,000 to $6,000 annually.

Use whatever resources are typical for establishing a reasonable wage for the work Mr. Brooks performs in the business. For estimation purposes, you may consider a temporary amount for your calculations. According to IRS data, the average S Corporation pays out about 40 percent of its income in the form of salary and 60 percent in the form of distributions. You will assess this in more detail during the formal planning phase, but you can see that there is at least a possibility for real savings.

The next topic is medical expenses. Virginia is working as a part-time bookkeeper and receives a salary. The problem with having the Brookses use an S Corporation to hold their software business is the tax laws prevent deductions of fringe benefits for the owners. This would mean they could not deduct their medical expenses through the business.

Viewing page one of the tax return, you can see that the Brooks family has medical expenses. Examining the tax return, you can see $9,200 in premiums, and they've said that they also pay about $2,800 in other out-of-pocket medical expenses. While the Brookses get the deduction for the premiums on page one, they're missing the $2,800 in other expenses altogether. Additionally, the medical-insurance premium isn't helping the Brookses save self-employment tax because it is only being used as a deduction for income tax.

Using an S Corporation won't help the Brookses deduct the fringe benefits. Therefore, there may be a significant reason to maintain a Schedule C as a means of recognizing this deduction. The business purpose for the sole proprietorship might be for one of the two business functions in the Brookses software business. Utilizing a Schedule C provides the opportunity to allow Mr. Brooks to hire Virginia to work as a bookkeeper in that Schedule C business in exchange for medical benefits. In fact, implementing a medical-expense reimbursement plan may provide an excellent way to maximize the deductions for both the medical premiums and the out-of-pocket medical expenses. As a result, the Brookses would take the deduction on Schedule C as an employee benefit expense, and that will save them about $2,200 a year in taxes.

Next, the son, William, who will be taking over the business, comes into play. Currently, William is paid a salary, and you will notice from the information given in his tax return that he is missing out on some deductions by earning his income as an employee. We know that Howard and Virginia plan on transitioning the business to William. The Brookses might consider bringing William into the business and gifting some shares of the S Corporation to him. William can do some tax planning of his own now, and the business would save some self-employment taxes. Thus, William can be a shareholder of the S Corporation, split his earnings between a lower, reasonable wage and distributions, and save self-employment tax on the pass-through distribution. Doing this would save about $7,400 in tax. It also opens up a whole new world of opportunities for William, so that he can do some tax planning of his own. Remember, we know that he has some significant medical expenses. Can we do something with those expenses in terms of the Schedule C?

What about the issue of retirement? Could the Brooks family do a simple IRA for Virginia and take that deduction through the Schedule C to create some more self-employment savings? In reality, the Brooks family could contribute $12,000 plus a $2,500 catch-up contribution since the parents are over 50 years old. Another $14,500 in their retirement account in a simple IRA will save them about $2,000 per year.

The True Value of Selling Planning Services

Although you now know the key elements to selling planning services, your knowledge is not helpful unless you can effectively communicate the value of the services to your clients. Therefore, the key ingredients for selling engagements at premium fees—the magic of communicating your premium fees to clients—is to always quote your fees in context to the value that you bring, which is the savings you have created for your clients. For example, in the Brooks family case study, if you are trying to sell the Brooks family a tax plan for $7,000, you may want to approach them with the following verbiage:

> "Mr. and Mrs. Brooks, I've got some good news, and I've got bad news. The bad news is you're wasting about $10,000 to $16,000 each year in taxes that you just don't have to pay. The good news is you don't need to do that anymore; you just need a better plan. I can do the work that it takes to help you keep that money. The fee is just a one-time charge of $7,000, and you'll be able to take home $10,000 to $16,000, by my estimation, every year after that. That means that in the next five years, your bank account will increase by $50,000! When can you get in here to get started?"

By communicating this way, you're doing a couple of things:

- You're directing the attention to the value that you are bringing and the potential savings within the tax plan.
- You're directing the attention to what the clients want. The clients want money; they don't want a form or a vague price of how much it's going to cost them.

In my experience with the real-life "Brooks family," the time it took me to explain the tax plan totaled about an hour and a half. I spent about two and half to three hours preparing the plan and preparing for the session. Finally, I spent 30 minutes following up with them afterwards. In total, you are facing about five, six, or even seven hours of your time by the time you add in the initial estimate. Let's say your hourly billing rate is $300. If you tie in the amount of time you would spend on tax-planning services like I did with the "Brooks family," $2,000 would be the reflective engagement fee. However, I charged $7,000 for that plan. That is a lot nicer than $2,000, and it still leaves the client feeling happy about their decision.

Seven thousand dollars is more than the client is used to paying, but when you contrast this fee to the value that you're bringing them, the fee is not shocking. In this real-life scenario, I ended up selling two tax plans because the son was brought in for part of the session. He loved what we were doing for his mother and father and wanted to experience savings as well. Bringing him in as a business owner provided opportunities for him and offered the chance for me to sell a second tax plan.

Again, you must focus on the value, both when you're selling the plan, and when you're billing for ongoing work. What does ongoing work mean? You start out by selling a tax plan, and eventually you must also address compliance needs. If a client doesn't require a significant amount of changes, there is not enough to warrant a brand-new plan at some point in the future, so you will assume maintenance mode; you're simply maintaining that plan.

That being said, you still need to direct the client's focus to the value that you bring when you bill for ongoing work. In my practice, I still redirect that focus to the value that I've brought to the relationship, even if it was a year or two ago and I'm merely billing for a tax return. In fact, I feature this total savings amount right on the invoice. I run two versions of the tax return both with and without the tax-planning advice. I do this despite how old it is because it's my expertise that helps create that saving year after year. Then, I present the amount that I'm charging them for the tax return. Always remember to focus on that value.

Presenting Planning Engagements to Your Clients

Communicating the value of tax planning and savings to your clients should become a regular sales routine. I have probably given the speech

I gave to the "Brooks family" several hundred times to other clients. Be patient with yourself and allow yourself adequate practice time, so that you will improve each time you pitch a planning engagement.

Aside from just practicing your pitch, you should be prepared to respond to objections. The reality with any sales pitch is that not everyone says "yes." However, this doesn't mean that a "no" is final. When you practice overcoming objections, you might be able to persuade a "no" into a "yes." Remember, every client is different and requires a unique approach. Your main advantage is that despite the fact that your fees are higher than most people are used to paying for tax services, your clients perceive they haven't been offered this much value in the past.

If clients object to your asking price, redirect their focus to the value that you are bringing them. If Mr. Brooks says, "Well, that's way too much. You charged me significantly less than that for my tax return," you can respond with "Well, I could charge you less, Mr. Brooks, but I've identified $50,000 here in wasted taxes. I wouldn't want to cut out any of my work. I'd like to get you the most savings possible. Is there a part of the $50,000 you would want me to leave out?" You're redirecting the focus to the value that you're bringing, and more often than not, the client wants to take advantage of that value to its fullest extent.

Practicing your pitch should also extend to reacting to procrastinators. We are all familiar with procrastinators—the people who always say they will get back to you at a later time. Again, when dealing with these people, redirect their focus to the potential value. For example, you might say, "Mr. Brooks, the longer that you wait, the less we're going to be able to do, and you're not going to be able to save the full $16,000 this year. Let's get this done now, so your next tax payment, which is due on June 15, will be much smaller."

Notice how I redirected his focus and highlighted the possible savings in my example. Here, again, you must emphasize your value to get paid what you're worth.

CHAPTER 8

Cherry-Picking Clients and Identifying Opportunities

One of the benefits of changing your business model to highlight your value to customers is that it really distinguishes you in the marketplace. In fact, in most cases, so few tax businesses operate this way that it's possible to completely eliminate your competition. Consider a situation when you are perceived as the only advisor offering true tax reductions—demand for your services will explode!

The benefit of enjoying high demand for your service is that it allows you to be picky about whom you choose to work with. Imagine being in a position to handpick your clients, to work only with people you actually enjoy, to work with those who happily pay your fees—on time. Imagine eliminating all the hassle of disorganized taxpayers who wait until the last minute to remit their work, or who find other ways to make your life more difficult. When you build a successful business where you get paid what you're worth, you can cherry-pick great clients and let the rest go.

The logical question is how to decide whom to work with and whom to let go. The goal of this chapter is for you to master the concept of cherry-picking clients. When choosing clients, you'll develop a wish list of client characteristics and then evaluate the clients against those traits. This will allow you to create a plan to identify your "pink-slip list" and replace your lowest-ranking clients. Even better, it will define what you want from clients in the future, and ensure you'll get paid what you're worth.

The Client Rating System

Have you ever developed client acceptance criteria? Most tax business owners, and entrepreneurs in general, readily accept any business that comes through the door. It's funny to see when someone's list of criteria contains only the word "breathing."

It's important to adopt some formalized process to evaluate your current and prospective clients because how else will you know that you are a good fit?

Dominique's Story

When I started my business, I was fortunate that my failure to have a marketing plan did not hurt my ability to get new clients. Referrals, website, and foot traffic helped propel my business to the high volumes I thought I needed at the time to earn what I'm worth. However, once I decided to focus on my tax-planning expertise, it became apparent that I didn't need the majority of my workload anymore. In fact, the waiting list for my next available strategy appointment was so extensive that it became difficult to decide whom I'd like to fit into my schedule and whom I'd place on the waiting list. I realized I needed some sort of formal rating system that I could use, and that I could delegate to my team to assist with evaluating people to see if they were still a good fit for the new direction of my business.

I began to list the qualities of a good client that fit well with my company vision, culture, and values. Once I built the list, I realized I needed some method for scoring clients against a standard, which, once implemented, made it easy to have my staff rate each project and client. This became our client acceptance criteria. For those who did not appear to be a good fit, I made personal referrals to other tax accountants in town. (This is why it's important to get to know your competition. You never know when you can refer business. Over the years, I have received tax-planning cases from my "competition," and we have a great working relationship.)

Lesson Learned: Building a great business also means choosing whom you want to surround yourself with each day. Aside from measuring the success rates of your marketing, leads, and profits, it is important to measure your happiness factor. Exercising this habit creates empowerment and confidence and ensures a successful business.

I've made the client evaluation tool I use available online for free. To get your own copy, simply visit **www.GetPaidForYourWorth.com** and start using it in your business!

In developing your own list, you should consider the types of engagements you enjoy working on, the potential for additional business, and the opportunity to work with key influencers in your target market. How likable is the person? Do you enjoy working together? Categorizing opportunities with evaluations like these allows you to notice trends, similarities, and characteristics that help you to clearly define your vision.

Here are a few examples of things you might consider in developing your evaluation criteria:

1. How much do you enjoy working with the client?
2. Is the client a good source of referrals?
3. How well organized is the client?
4. Does the client expose the firm to liability?
5. Is there an opportunity for growth with this client?

My Client Rating System assigns grades A, B, C, or D to each taxpayer. If a client scores between 60 and 69 points, then he or she is a

D-grade client. You may be surprised to learn how many of your clients fall under this category. When I first used this assessment, I was so afraid to get rid of the clients who were considered D-grade. Even though I didn't want to work with them, I still was fearful of losing that income. However, I looked at the big picture: losing D-grade clients allows you to gain A-grade work. Once you replace the D-grade clients, you'll feel great because you're able to surround yourself with people that you want to work with and replace low fees with higher fees.

I also began to realize that these D-grade clients cost me the time my A-grade clients deserved. The problem with D-grade clients is they tend to be very needy! While I'm busy trying to please the unpleasable "D's", my loyal "A's" are quietly waiting for me to become available.

Consider evaluating clients based on how much you like them. Determine whether or not they are helping you build your business by bringing in referrals. Look at things like how closely related people in your business are to key clients. Your Client Rating System should also examine the value of clients based on fees. It should prompt important questions, such as these:

- How often does the firm sell services to the client?
- Does the client pay his or her fees on time?
- What percentage of total firm revenue does the client represent?

Another asset the Client Rating System offers is the chance for you to look at a client's opportunity for growth. With this system, you can predict whether you're going to be able to sell more services to this client, or if he or she is on the way out.

Again, the idea behind the Client Rating System is for you to go in and score your clients and identify which clients should be replaced.

Locating Core Clients

Let's look at where you can find potential clients, so that you can build your own pipeline. You want to find streams of clients that allow you to pick and choose whom you really want to work with. Instead of taking anyone who comes along, you will refer to the Client Rating System to identify your ideal and core client. Take only the types of clients who allow you to become more efficient at what you do. This will allow you to tailor your marketing message, which is another secret to building a hugely successful practice.

Seminars

Seminars on tax planning are a great source of identifying potential clients. Any time you speak to a room full of people, you cut down on the amount of time required to spend with each person; you maximize the amount of people you can reach with just one pitch. Participating in seminars with the right forum can help build your credibility and your connection with your audience.

This is when knowing your target market is so critical. If you don't have a target market, identify one. Before you can participate in seminars, ensure that you're speaking to your target market to optimize the marketing potential. Whenever you can get in front of your ideal market through a speaking engagement, do so. Seminars are a very effective way to increase your leads.

Referrals

A second way to locate core clients is by implementing a system for referrals. I'm sure you've received referrals from clients in the past, but it is very important to control these referrals by systematizing. Controlling referrals includes having the right kind of referrals coming in at appropriate times. For example, establish processes for how you respond to prospective clients' inquiries. Consider mailing marketing materials to referrals. Establishing procedures for how your staff responds to inquiries can help maintain the current schedule while responding to new business in a timely and appropriate fashion.

Networking and Social Media

I believe networking and social media complement each other. When I use the term networking, I mean more traditional methods, such as association groups, referral groups, or any other type of social events. Social media, however, is networking through the Internet, including Twitter, LinkedIn, and Facebook. Whether you choose to network physically or utilize social media, make sure these activities and platforms are used by your target market. Proper networking can be an extremely effective way to increase your leads.

If you're not currently using social media in your business, I recommend that you start. Take advantage of any resources available that teach you how to use it effectively. Watch a YouTube video on how to correctly use social media. Look it up on Google. I'm not just talking about putting a page on LinkedIn, Twitter, or Facebook and hoping people will find you. There's a proactive methodology to it, and how people are using social media to advance their businesses and brands is an important part of your overall marketing strategy. You can also consider hiring a specialist to teach you about social media or to manage social media presence.

Existing Clients

Seminars, referrals, and networking trends are all great ideas for looking for new clients, but your existing client list can be a tremendous asset to you as well. In fact, I spoke with a Certified Tax Coach recently who found 45 tax-planning engagements all at $2,500 each just by going through his existing clients. Don't overlook this goldmine—it's the easiest place to start, and it's how I began building my A-grade client list. Turning to your existing clients provides security because these are people that you already know and enjoy working with, and most likely they have friends with similar qualities.

Announce your "new" tax-planning service to your clients. I'm saying "new" because this service is new to them. Treating this as a separate engagement is a new service. If you send newsletters or client emails, write about your "new" services. It will get your clients' attention and start conversations; clients will start asking you about these "new" services. You can also ask permission from one of your good clients to run a story in your newsletter about what you were able to do for them—a testimonial. For example, I saved Mr. Brooks $16,000 with a tax plan. You'll quickly realize your phone is ringing more often than before.

Catering to Your Clients' Wants

A sad fact is that while people will pay you for things that they need, they're not too happy or excited to do so. Because of this, you will get inquires from a lot of price shoppers. These are the people who are looking for the best deal in town because they really wish they didn't have to do it at all. This might be the tone you hear from a majority of your prospective clients, and it probably strikes a chord with you. Your clients just don't want to deal with paying taxes, but, legally, they must. This section is going to show you how to turn a product that you offer from something your clients need into something they want. When you start selling something that they want, a remarkable thing happens: they become willing to pay premium fees and work on your terms because it's something that they're happy about. It's something that excites them.

"The Nordstrom Way of Conducting Business"

Converting existing clients to your pricing structure is something I call "The Nordstrom Way of Conducting Business." The first thing I would like to point out is that clients will treat you the way that you train them to treat you. Therefore, consider communicating that you are making some changes in your firm. You can approach clients and say something like, "Mr. and Mrs. Brooks, our focus is changing to other ways we can save you money, so we're changing the way that we fulfill our services, and the way we deliver our services to valued clients like you."

The reason I refer to this method as "The Nordstrom Way of Conducting Business" is because Nordstrom's customers don't take merchandise up to the counter to negotiate the price, attempt to take the merchandise without paying, or to ask to set up a layaway plan. Nordstrom conducts business a certain way—with the highest standards—and their customers accept that. Nordstrom's approach to conducting business is exactly what you have to do in your business if you want to change the way that you're working with your current clients.

Bundling Services

As mentioned previously, you should consider bundling services. For instance, you can combine tax planning and tax return preparation into one package. I have successfully done this in my practice in the past and will continue to do so. In fact, dividing the annual cost by 12, converting it into a monthly fee, helps to ease the financial burden on the client. I've been doing this very successfully for years. I mentioned that I no longer include the tax plan as part of the tax return preparation services, and that's because I noticed that when I did it separately, my clients paid a little more attention; they actually implemented the ideas that I was sharing with them. Bundling services is yet another way to distinguish yourself in the marketplace.

Measuring the Value of a Client to Your Firm

Do you know the real value of a client to your business? When marketing, truly understanding what you can afford to invest in marketing tactics depends on the value of a client. Thus, in order to calculate the average value of a client, you need to know how long the average life of that relationship is. Ask yourself this:

- What is your attrition rate?
- How long do your typical clients remain clients?

If you're in the "quick refund" market, the lifetime of a client may be short, so you would express the average life in terms of months. However, if you have high-level planning clients, the average lifespan may be decades. There are several ways you can determine the lifespan of a client, including, but not limited to, the following:

- Look at when the client first became a client
- Look through physical records
- Refer to operations software or your tax return preparation software

Next, calculate the average value for each client. You may want to divide your clients by service type. For this calculation, take your total annual revenues by service type and divide by the number of clients requiring that service. This equation reveals the average annual revenue per client. Then, simply multiply that factor by the average relationship age of your client. This gives you a loose representation of the average value of a client to your business. You can use this information to determine how much money may be worthwhile to spend on average to get a new client or to retain that client. Figure 8.1 demonstrates this formula.

Figure 8.1 Client Value Calculation

Total Annual Revenues by Service Type:	$_____
÷ Total Clients Requiring Service:	#_____
= Average Annual Revenue per Client:	$_____
x Average Life of Client:	_____
= Average Value of Client:	$_____

Always apply marketing approaches to your existing clients to retain them. Remember, your existing clients are valuable to your business, and you should be marketing proactively to them as well as to prospective clients. There are numerous ways you can market to existing clients in a leveraged way, such as:

- Newsletters
- Promotions
- Seminars
- Emails or personal notes

When you know the value of a client to your firm, you're able to make more educated decisions about investing in marketing. For example, if you know the average value of a client to your firm is $15,000, you can conclude that spending a large amount of money to keep a client or to acquire new ones may be worthwhile.

And face it: when you get paid what you're worth, it's worth investing a little to make a lot!

CHAPTER 9

Maintaining the Health of Your Tax Business

Thus far, I've reiterated the importance of self-assessment and -evaluation to determine where you currently are in your tax practice, and where you plan to be. This chapter is going to talk about all the different places that you're going to look in your business to see what's working and what's not working. This will also help you work with your clients in a more consultative way, which opens up the door to charging premium fees for coaching. Thus, what I'm about to share with you is not only important for the health of your own business, but it will also assist you in going that extra mile for your clients.

The success of your tax business really depends on taking its temperature throughout its lifecycle. There are certain elements of your business that you need to routinely check to confirm that you're on the right track and offering the best services possible.

If you want to transform your business or make improvements to it without a plan, you're going to get stuck and possibly overwhelmed. Therefore, before you make any changes, consider a health checklist. Creating such a list for your company will help you evaluate the progress toward your business goals. Creating a business health checklist for your clients will add more value to your relationship and provide additional services to offer and include in your monthly fixed price agreements.

This is an opportunity to check in and deeply evaluate your business. As you're reading this chapter, have a pen and notebook ready. Take this time to evaluate your business sincerely and open yourself to implementing some new ideas.

Tax Business Health Checklist

Before you start creating your business health checklist, follow these rules:

Do not chastise yourself if

- you haven't done this before, or if
- you can't accomplish everything immediately.

It's going to take you some time to really think about your business. The strategies that I'm going to share with you are going to enable you to do just that. Give yourself a slight break and don't regret not having changed previously. Start where you are currently and move forward—and be at peace with the process.

Consider creating a business dashboard that will give you visibility over your business. You can customize this however you like, and I encourage you to do so. Figure 9.1 features a dashboard worksheet.

What does a dashboard offer you? It gives you information. It's an instrument panel with tools to help you navigate your path to grow your business. It serves as a GPS, showing you where you're going and where you've been. Without your dashboard, you are driving blindly—or worse, perhaps you're not in the driver's seat at all. This is a good time to ask yourself, "Who's driving my business?"

The largest benefit of implementing a dashboard is that it gives you visibility; you can see where you're going. If you can create your dashboard in a systematized, leveraged way, you can get this information at a moment's notice. You can still meet all your deadlines and those tight client commitments. Yet, you take an active role in navigating your business. This is especially important during tax season when you just don't have time to spend on your own financial analysis.

Figure 9.1 Dashboard Worksheet

Tax Business Dashboard

Business Plan
Key Indicator #1 _____
Key Indicator #2 _____
Key Indicator #3 _____

Happiness Factor (gauge: 5, 10, 15, 20, 25, 30, 35)

Business Finances
Financials within 1 month? ☐ Yes ☐ No
Budget? ☐ Yes ☐ No
% Year to date compared to Prior Year _____

Products and Services
Product Mix: revenues as a % by service line

Service #	% of Revenues
1	
2	
3	
4	
5	

Avg. Rev / Product: _____

Marketing Campaign Results

Campaign #	Revenues	Cost	ROI %
1			
2			
3			
4			
5			

Retention Cost: _____
Retained Revenues: _____
ROI: _____ %

Client Satisfaction
Value of a Client
Average Life of a Client _____
X
Average Revenues Per Client _____ = _____
Satisfaction Rating (per surveys) _____

Efficiency and Delegation
Firm Profit Margin: _____
Staff Profitability =
Payroll Expenses _____ /
Revenues from Staff _____
Avg. Project Realization: _____

One other notable benefit from an efficient dashboard is that it helps your clients. I've mentioned the quandary that we have as tax practitioners with the vicious cycle of getting paid for transactions. You can use the financial dashboard to take a coaching role with your clients. Working as a business advisor really changes the relationship that you have with your clients, so that they focus on your worth. Instead of being paid for preparing forms, you'll get paid for your expertise, the coaching, and the relationship that you have with your clients. This is the kind of structured information that you can use to coach their way to a better business. It's the kind of work that you can charge premium fees for and use to attract new business.

These are the seven areas of a good tax business health checklist:

1. **The Overall Quality of Your Business Life.** When you're a small-business owner, how you manage your business is important to your quality of life. Because you own the business, the quality of your business life affects your overall outlook on life. Work is where you spend the majority of your time, and what you sacrifice other areas of your life for. Thus, it makes total sense to monitor how you see the quality of your professional life.
2. **Business Planning.** Most business owners develop a business plan and put it away on a shelf or on a hard drive. Business planning in its truest sense comes alive when you regularly review and adjust your plan.
3. **Key Financial Indicators.** Your financial indicators are the milestones you will measure on your path to growth and development and help you focus on the most important numbers in your business that predict future success.
4. **Services.** The core of your business and its ability to generate income depends on your primary services and on how you price them.
5. **Marketing Success.** As you can imagine, this is a big area because if you don't market well, it can change your whole business outcome. Marketing is your ability to get in front of your target audience in the most favorable way to sell your core services.
6. **Customer Service and Client Satisfaction.** This measures how your clients feel about what you do, and whether they will continue to buy from you and refer others to you.

7. **Efficiency.** This is my favorite area because the ability to leverage your business and earn income even while you're not in the office depends on your ability to systematize your office and delegate work to be done in an efficient and effective manner to increase your profit margins. Doing so enables you to focus on the higher-end activities in your business, use your time more effectively, and improve overall profitability for you and for your clients.

All seven areas will ultimately increase the value of your business.

The Overall Quality of Your Business Life

First, examine the quality of your business life, which I refer to as your happiness factor. To start, ask yourself the following questions:

- What is the predominate feeling that I have toward my business and toward my clients?
- Am I happy?
- Am I satisfied at the end of each day?
- Do I feel overwhelmed?
- How do I feel towards the clients that I serve?

The bottom line is you need to know, acknowledge, and measure how you feel about your business on a regular basis.

In your evaluation, you should ask yourself about the predominate feeling you have toward your business. List all of the specific areas that please and displease you. Then, ask yourself about time, for example:

- Do you have time after work to spend with the people you care about or to do the things that you enjoy?
- Is your business giving you the quality of life that you want?
- When was the last time you took a day off to enjoy life? Can you afford to take time off, or do you feel guilty when you do?

Sometimes, the best changes that you can make are as simple as taking off Friday afternoons or transitioning away from clients you're unhappy with. You might focus on attracting more of the kind of clients you really enjoy working with—perhaps you identify that you really like to serve a certain group of people. Thinking about how you currently feel is very important because you can't change things you are unaware of. Including this in your tax business dashboard is a vital step toward evaluating your business.

Psychologists have said that it's possible to measure your happiness. One of the most important influences on happiness is social relationships; people who score high on life satisfaction tend to have close and supportive family and friends, and that includes coworkers and clients. You spend the majority of your time with coworkers and clients, so it makes a difference whether you enjoy their company. On the other hand, people who don't have close, enjoyable relationships with family and friends are likely to be unhappy.

Another key ingredient to happiness is to have important goals and to make progress toward those goals. For many people, it's important to feel a connection to something larger than yourself, and these are all things you should consider when you're evaluating your happiness factor.

When someone enjoys his or her work—whether it's paid or unpaid—they feel that it's meaningful and important, and that contributes to their business satisfaction. Now, I'm not encouraging you at all to do any work unpaid. Yet, when you work on things that you're passionate about, your overall business satisfaction increases. Perhaps you're doing some charity work, or maybe there's a hobby that you enjoy. These interests contribute to your business satisfaction. And if you can get paid well for those things, it makes it that much better; it's icing on the cake. On the other side, when work is going poorly, it can lower your business satisfaction.

One of the other issues is failing to make adequate progress towards goals, which can lead to business dissatisfaction. Thus, making progress toward goals helps you feel satisfied. Now, there is not one key to business satisfaction, but rather it's a recipe that includes a number of ingredients. With time and persistent work, your business satisfaction can improve. People who've had a loss recover over time. If you've had dissatisfying relationships or work, you can make changes over time that will increase your happiness.

Since defining your happiness is so important, I have based a quick happiness-factor test on a test designed by psychology professor Ed Diener from the University of Illinois. The point of this test is to really help you check in with the things that affect your happiness level and to start to make changes, so that you can make improvements and feel more satisfied. To find out your Happiness Factor, refer to the five statements in Figure 9.2 and decide whether you agree or disagree with each using a scale of one to seven (one is for strongly disagreeing; seven for strongly agreeing).

Figure 9.2 Happiness Factor Test

Happiness Factor

Decide whether you agree or disagree with each of the following statements by answering each on a scale of 1-7 where:
1 – completely disagreeing with the statement, and
7 – complete agreement with the statement.

- In most ways my business is ideal

1	2	3	4	5	6	7
○	○	○	○	○	○	○

- I enjoy the staff and clients I work with most of the time

1	2	3	4	5	6	7
○	○	○	○	○	○	○

- I am satisfied with my business

1	2	3	4	5	6	7
○	○	○	○	○	○	○

- So far I have gotten the important things I want in my business

1	2	3	4	5	6	7
○	○	○	○	○	○	○

- If I could start my business over, I would change almost nothing

1	2	3	4	5	6	7
○	○	○	○	○	○	○

Total your score and divide by 5 to calculate your happiness factor

My happiness factor is: _____

To understand your Happiness factor score, it's helpful to understand some of the components that go into most people's experience of happiness as discussed above.

Once you've answered all the questions, you can add up your score and divide by five. This score represents your Happiness Factor, which is good for measuring changes over time. The factor becomes a benchmark for you; you're comparing yourself against your own progress, which is what's most important.

Business Planning

Do you have a written business plan? I'm not talking about a 400-page business plan that's bound in leather with a gold foil stamp. I'm talking about maybe three pages of action items or bullet points or even a one-page business plan. Also:

- Have you written down who your market is and what you offer them?
- Have you written down your clients' primary concerns?
- Have you documented your budget and your marketing plan?
- Do you know where you want your business to be a year from today?

These are all questions that should be considered because business planning is central to making decisions.

I work with a lot of small business owners. I do coaching and consulting, and a big problem faced by these clients is the feeling of being overwhelmed; they can't make a decision because they don't know what they want. They don't know where they're headed. The minute they resolve these questions, decision making becomes simple, and implementation becomes possible. A written business plan helps to give you clarity and serves as a guide to help you remain clear about your vision and continue progressing from where you are now to where you'd like to be.

There's an old cliché that a goal is just a dream unless you write it down. A business plan is just a set of goals and action items to accomplish those goals. It acts as a roadmap to help you navigate to where you're trying to go.

Do you have a regular system for evaluating the essential components of your business and establishing action plans? Promote yourself from an employee to an investor in your business. I recommend updating your strategic plans quarterly—regular updates ensure you are continually progressing toward a higher level of business ownership. If you really want something to change, you've got to do something differently—you've got to get regular feedback and ideas to keep you progressing. Be sure to include accountability to make sure you follow through with what is important to you.

What kind of business are you building? Identifying the type of business—quantitatively and qualitatively—and defining your role in the business give you a clear picture of where you are headed.

What separates someone with decades of experience as a business owner from someone who owns an investor-owned business? Routinely creating and adjusting strategic plans and realizing those plans help you to work on the business rather than just in it.

Figure 9.3 Key Indicators for Business Planning

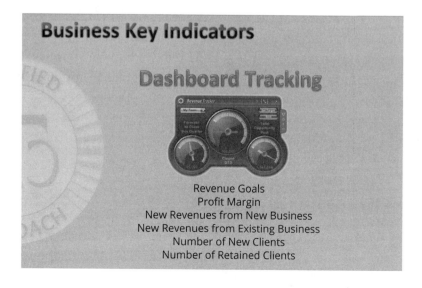

Identifying key indicators provides a way of measuring your success. The exact indicators depend on what the most important functions are in your business development. One idea is to look at the "budget-to-actual comparison." How do you measure up against your business plan? Your financial projections serve as your budget. A business plan will remind you what you need to accomplish in terms of revenue goals, for example.

You also want to consider your profit margin. Again, when comparing your actual performance to your business plan, you determine how you measure up. Factor in revenue from new business. Ask the following questions:

- What is your growth rate?
- Are you on target with your business plan?
- Do you have a revenue goal in mind?
- What about new revenues from existing business?
- Are you actively marketing new products and services to your existing clients?

As I pointed out previously, your existing client base is a treasure trove that's often overlooked. You should be actively promoting new ideas and services, so that you can increase your revenues.

You might want to track the total number of new clients either in revenues, quantity, or total number of tax plans or returns, for example. Whatever is important to you should be reflected in your business plan. We all have different reasons for why we have goals in mind. Perhaps you want to hit the million-dollar mark in your practice, or you want to have 1,000 clients. If these are meaningful goals to you, they should be recorded in your business plan for future reference and be monitored regularly for improvements.

Key Financial Indicators

The first question to ask yourself is whether or not you have a central location where you can quickly access financial information about your company. What I mean by this is: Do you have your financial information recorded in a dashboard like the one you're working on right now? My second question is: Do you use systems to help you record this data, so that you can produce it quickly?

We all have core competencies. I'm sure you're perfectly capable of entering your own accounting data into QuickBooks or other accounting software, but is this type of work the highest and best use of your time? Perhaps you're not doing it at all because you just don't have the time. Delegating this work is important because it means it will be done. Allowing someone to complete this work for you allows you to review the numbers in a meaningful way without spending all your available time just preparing your financial reports. Consider bringing in an outside service provider if you don't want your staff knowing your business finances. You can't intentionally improve what you don't measure, and measuring doesn't mean cramming it all in, so you can prepare your tax return on September 14. If you don't look at your numbers, except once a year when taxes are due, you do not have any chance to repair what may be broken.

Being busy is not a valid excuse why you're not measuring your finances. You must systematize the process, so that you have at least a bird's eye view, even during your busiest times. Weekly or, at the very least, monthly reporting can tell you how you're doing, and if things aren't going well, you can start to make changes right away—so don't wait until it gets out of hand.

Some of the subsequent areas for your business dashboard depend on your ability to produce financial data. Therefore, you can't produce financial data months after the fact; you need to know that information in real time, so that you can make meaningful decisions.

In regard to your financial information, don't be afraid of that suspense account. If you can't fully reconcile because there's missing information or your bookkeeper has questions about posting, it's okay to review later on. Use a holding space so that you can close the month and get the information you need. I think accountants, because of our personalities, tend to let our need for perfection stop us from creating real progress. Let me tell you, holding onto that fear will keep you from having the business that you truly want to have. There's nothing wrong with using a parking place to get your accounting records done; you can come back later to perfect it if you prefer.

Do you know how much you're normally spending every month? You should have an expense budget as well for things like wages and marketing, etc. This includes your common monthly expenses. Do you have the budget written down, and do you stick to it? This is especially helpful in times of frenzy because you don't have to evaluate based on an estimate. You can just look at your budget, and if it's not consistent, you can reject it or accept it, depending on where you're at financially.

I realize this seems so simple, especially for our profession. You're probably even telling your clients that they need to do this. But do you do it yourself in your business? I want you to have a clear idea of what your monthly expenses are. What are some of those one-off expenses, like a new computer? Do you have a budget for that? Do you stick to it? Do you say, "This is my budget, and I'm not going to go over because if I do, I'm not going to be profitable"?

The next questions are very important. Do you have enough cash coming into your business every month to support your expenses beyond overhead? Are you living the lifestyle you want? Can you afford the lifestyle you want? Does your business provide that? If things are tight, but you know that an influx of cash is coming, do you have a place where you can get low-cost financing, so that you can continue to grow your business? And better yet, do you have a solid plan for creating monthly recurring revenue? If you don't, get one. It's a great way to even out the cash flow, so that you can afford your business expenses and the lifestyle that you want.

The next indicator is revenue. Ask yourself if your revenue is increasing every year. Do you compare last year to this year? Do you spend time looking at it every year to see if your business is increasing? And if it is increasing, at what pace? Is growth rate consistent with your future plans?

More important than gross revenues is profit. Did you make enough profit to support your lifestyle? Do you know which of your products and services are the most profitable? Do you really know where you're making your money? Are your profit margins changing? Do you compare year to year, so you can see the trends?

Product and Service Offerings

Sticking with the theme of finances, examine product and service offerings. When looking at whether or not your business is healthy, you've got to examine your services. A big question is whether you offer real value to your clients. Are they getting what they want and need from you to either solve their problem or move toward fulfilling a dream? This is simple to overlook in a tax business because you may consider your services as offering tax returns.

If you want to get paid what you're worth, you also need to ask yourself if you have a system for regularly communicating your value to your clients. Do your clients know how much you've saved them over the years? Don't be shy in communicating this important information to your customers—it can lead to better referrals as well; when your clients know exactly how much you've done for them, they are better qualified to tell someone else why your services are special.

When building a business focused on value, routinely tracking average value created is a vital financial indicator. Not only does this assist the entire team with working together toward a common goal, it helps in your marketing message as well!

Identifying which projects are more profitable is important for evaluating your performance. It's important to track your revenues and costs per service, so you can measure the efficiency of the fulfillment and the popularity of the service and identify the services you may consider canceling or modifying to improve your performance.

Similar to efficiency is effectiveness. When considering price, one of the things to examine is the return on investment for your clients. As such, routinely measuring your effectiveness as a firm keeps you focused on the single greatest factor in the business: your value.

Without a listing of your core products and services, you can really lose touch with what is most popular, which will be discussed later. Focus on delivering what your clients are demanding, what you are excellent at doing, as well as what is considered most valuable to your family of customers.

Here's something to consider: sometimes, a service that you offer is not valuable anymore because people can get it at a lower cost or for free. But you can still be of service and deliver value. As our lives continue to be busy, one of the ways you can offer real value to clients is to deliver information. Even if it is available for free on the Internet, you can compile information on a topic and present it to your clients as a step-by-step process that is simple and doable. You've cut out all the noise and simplified it for them, so they don't have to do that research themselves.

This leads back to the idea of getting paid for your expertise compared to getting paid for transactions. When you change the way you work with your clients, especially the way you charge for your value, you can charge premium fees because the client's perception is different. People pay you for your expertise and knowledge, not for the tasks you perform. So consider repackaging information. Perhaps you can consider doing a report or an eBook, or a seminar or webinar. Again, even if you don't charge for these services, it's added value for your clients. It's a great way to build loyalty.

I suggest tracking your average price per engagement and per client. This not only helps you with establishing minimum fees, which will help increase your overall revenues, but it's also an important factor in business valuation for tax practices. Most prospective tax business buyers want to know this information. The more you pay attention to this and work to increase it, the more valuable your firm becomes.

Another aspect of services and products is whether you know which of your services and products are the most popular. Have you been paying attention to how many of each product you sell? Let's say that you offer write-up work in addition to tax work, and maybe you have three

CHAPTER 9

different packages—one that includes payroll, one that includes consultations, and one that just includes reporting. Are you tracking each product line or package? Have you been paying attention to how many of each you're selling, so that you know which one is most popular?

Tracking your mix of services in terms of revenue will give you the ability to see what is selling, and how the numbers are changing, so that you can react—especially in times of a tough economy.

It's also wise to ask your clients or your target market what they want, and what they value. Don't just guess what people want—ask them. There are many wonderful free tools available online, such as Survey Monkey, or perhaps you can use your contact-management software to administer and summarize survey results. It won't take very long to set a survey up, and it won't take your clients long to reply.

Paying attention to the different needs of your audience can help you stay in touch with what to offer your clients—do market research. If you keep offering the same thing over and over, but your clients' needs have changed, you may miss out on important opportunities to add value. Engaging frequently with your audience is important. Being in touch with what clients want enables you to offer a new product or service line to meet the demand.

To recap what you should be monitoring on your dashboard under product and service offerings, consider the following:

- First, measure your product lines as a percentage of your revenues to see how you stack up, and you can identify trends. Use your tax preparation software and other tools to track the number of returns prepared.
- Use your dashboard in a leveraged way to get you the information that you need.
- Calculate the average fees per engagement and per client.

Complimentary Pricing Essentials Tool Kit

Includes:

Worksheets from this book

Price Increase Announcement Template

Price Increase Package Opt-In Certificate Template

Price Offer Opt-Out Certificate Template

Audit Protection Package Profit Analyzer

Get Paid What You're Worth Home Video Course

Just visit www.GetPaidForYourWorth.com

CHAPTER 10

Maintaining the Health of Your Tax Business—Getting (and Keeping) Clients

Marketing

Many tax professionals do very little formal marketing at all. With consumer needs exceeding the number of advisors approximately 7 to 1, most pros don't need to market to get clients. However, if you're looking to improve the type of clients you work with, and find quality, premium-fee clients, it may require some marketing.

When evaluating your marketing, consider the following sections:

- Planning
- Branding
- Implementation
- Lead generation
- Tracking
- Conversion

Do you have a written marketing plan? Do you keep a marketing calendar with your campaigns, your promotions, and what that marketing is going to consist of? What days of the week is that going to happen, for example? Do you put that on the same calendar that you do everything with? Do you include everything that you have to do to prepare to do those marketing tasks? I highly recommend it.

A marketing calendar can save you time and stress. In fact, it can really get you through the busiest of times. During the super-frenzied tax season, all you have to do is follow your marketing calendar, which was carefully and strategically developed when you actually had the soundness of mind to think about it. It's also easy to delegate with a marketing calendar. You can't delegate something that's in your head. Your administration team can take a clearly defined task calendar and execute it with very little direction from you while you're focused on more valuable things.

If your marketing plan is simply sticky notes attached to your computer, it is chaos, not a marketing plan. At least organize a file and keep everything in one place, so that you can get to it, and you can find it easily. I keep all of my ad copies, applications, and strategies in one place so that it's easily accessible both to me and my team. If a new opportunity comes up—even during tax season—I can pull our file and choose from something that I've already done before and not spend any extra time.

Your brand is an image that you use for your marketing methods and message. It's a reflection of who you are, and it communicates your clear expertise and specialties. When building your branding checklist, indicate whether or not you have thought through what your brand is. If you have a brand, do your marketing materials reflect your brand and image? What does your logo say about you? Do you have a logo? Do you use specific business colors, images, or fonts, for example? What is it that you want people to think about you and your company? What adjectives would someone use to describe you? Are they using the adjectives that you want them to use?

You can incorporate your brand on LinkedIn or any other social media site. You can change the way that your profile looks, and you can incorporate your branding. In doing so, you're creating an identity, and most accountants don't actually do this. If you can create a brand for yourself or adopt one that's done for you, you simply have no competition. It really eliminates most of the competition out there.

CHAPTER 10

The next area of marketing is implementation. You've planned and thought about your brand, but do you have a list of marketing techniques? What are you currently using, and are you marketing on a consistent basis? Are you out there every week doing some kind of marketing, or do you just market once a year? Marketing is a marathon, not a sprint. When your brand is consistently present in the marketplace, letting people know about you, you have a better chance of receiving new business.

It's not necessary to market aggressively. The purpose of marketing is just so that people know that you exist. It takes people hearing your message many times before they actually say yes. If you can get very effective at this and market on a consistent basis, you will see success. I know it can be frustrating sometimes, especially if you've invested a lot of money in a marketing technique that didn't work. It's easy to throw in the towel. But if you continue trying different techniques, you will start to see some results. It is difficult to improve what you don't measure. Track the success of the techniques you use and make decisions about them from the information that you get. Don't just throw in the towel after one attempt because it often takes many attempts before you discover what works for you.

Consider adding to your checklist your current marketing challenge for the year. Identify what you can do differently. Even though it might require you to stretch and grow, it can be a great experiment. Remember, it could fail. That's the problem with business. Yes, it involves risk; there's no guarantee. On the other hand, part of the reason why you're self-employed is that you like to reach your potential. Why not learn and try new marketing techniques?

The most important aspect of marketing is testing and measuring the success of your marketing techniques. Marketing is a lot like fishing. The art really comes from casting a wide net and getting one or two fish from each of your marketing strategies. You might not get 30 fish from one technique, but you can certainly catch two each from 15 different techniques. Cast your net and be sure to look inside that net to see if you've got something, or it might be time to move on to a new technique. Again, test and measure your results.

Consider marketing as an investment and look at it just like you would evaluate any other investment. Calculate the return you're receiving. Once you have this information at your fingertips, you can properly evaluate the results from your campaign, and you can determine if it's worthwhile to continue.

Some of the indicators you'll want to track are the number of leads you receive from a campaign and your conversion rate, which is your ability to convert those leads into paying clients. You'll also want to evaluate the quality of the leads and the quality of the sales you generate from each campaign.

Lastly, let's talk about the conversion section of the marketing area. Conversion measures how many leads from your pipeline actually become clients. This indicator can help you fine-tune your sales message. Again, it is difficult to know what to change if you don't measure key factors, and that includes looking at the one who got away. So track your conversion rates. If you're meeting with new prospects, for example, and you know that you're only converting one out of every ten prospects into clients, you can use that information to change what you're doing. Try doing something different and see if it improves your results!

Customer Service and Client Satisfaction

Customer service and client satisfaction are extremely crucial when maintaining your business' health. There are many tools out there to assist you with doing this easily and quickly. It's also an easy task to delegate.

- Do you track whether or not your clients are happy?
- Do you survey them?
- Do you ask your clients after every single tax engagement what their level of satisfaction is?

I give my clients an evaluation form after every service, and I ask them not only which of my services that they found most helpful but also what areas they favored the least. On my evaluations, I ask questions such as:

- If I were to do it all over again, what would you like me to add or take out?
- Have you found that this has been helpful to you?
- What was the best part of our meeting? What could we have done differently?
- Are you satisfied with the products and services you received?
- Would you mind providing a testimonial to help others understand how we are different?

Client satisfaction and customer service go hand in hand. This gives you insight into whether or not your clients are satisfied with your services. It's also an opportunity to handle complaints and questions that they may have. Additionally, asking for testimonials assists you with your product-offering mix. Finally, communicating with your clients and evaluating your performance opens up the personal relationship you have with your client and could help you improve your business.

Efficiency

The key to improving the profitability in your business using this model is monitoring and improving prices, revenues, effectiveness, efficiency, and delegation.

- Can you find things easily in your office?
- Can you do your work with minimal effort?
- What wastes your time?
- Are you as efficient as possible so that you can afford to focus on delivering the most value possible?
- Can you or your staff stay focused?
- Do you keep track of the tasks?
- Do you have a to-do list somewhere in writing?
- Are your profit margins continually improving?

Consider using operational software to keep track of processes and systems, and create automated processes using technology wherever you can.

Create an efficient system for your tasks. Whether you have systems right now or you want to implement new systems, when you begin systematizing, focus on the things that have the biggest financial impact on your business first.

Whether you select one of the operational tools on the market, or even if you use a centrally stored spreadsheet, maintaining a master list of tasks leads to improved delegation and efficiency, which allows you and your team to focus on what is most important to your clients.

If you're not fully comfortable allowing people to make changes that might affect your priority list, determine the cost of maintaining control over this area. How much is this behavior costing you?

Another way to identify the most important processes to systematize is to look at the things that cause you the most pain. Creating a solution to alleviate the pain in your office should lead to improved efficiency.

When considering staff efficiency and effectiveness, much can be shared and taught far beyond the space I have in this book. To get excellent results and quality from your staff, it's important to establish processes and systems for hiring and retaining top talent. More information can be learned on this topic in *Extreme Staff Makeover: Attracting, Hiring, Managing and Keeping Top Talent for Your Tax Business*.

List the ways to measure your desired results and hold the players accountable. Consider implementing evaluations for each and every project. This makes employee reviews much easier. Engagement evaluations hold your team accountable. It gives real-time feedback, so that everyone can correct and improve their performance. Set value goals and clearly communicate your expectations to your staff. Clear communication alleviates a lot of misunderstandings and miscommunications later on.

In building your business dashboard, include tracking staff profitability. Profit margins are an important key performance indicator to measure. You may think that profit margins do not exist in a tax business because it's service oriented, but they do. Consider that goods are services that we offer to our clients. The cost of goods sold includes wages, benefits, and other expenses such as e-filing fees. I highly recommend calculating profit margins and effectiveness (client ROI) for each and every project. It allows clear communication and goals for your staff, and it's a great way to get your staff to do what you really want them to do.

I've covered a lot of information in regard to the dashboard and the health checklist, so before I conclude, I want to share with you the five things that I feel like you have to do first. These items should be the highest priority on your checklist:

1. **Systematize your finances.** If you're not making a profit, you're going to be out of business. Period. Your finances have to be the highest priority for you. Get your financial house in order, including your business and your marketing plan. Stop running your business by the seat of your pants. Write everything down and systematize your office. The clarity that comes from these processes is amazing. Work on your business plan as well.

2. **Apply effective marketing strategies.** Stop and figure out which marketing techniques bring you the most business and stop using techniques that are not working for you. Attempt new techniques that may do better. But figure out which ones are the strongest for you now.

3. **Join a network.** If you're doing it all on your own, it can be very expensive and can take you a long time. Have a support network of your peers that you can rely on to get new ideas. Pay attention to what is creating new business and ask your clients, so that you know what marketing and products they're interested in.

4. **Start using a marketing calendar.** Create a single place where you enter your monthly tasks, so that all you have to do is either delegate the tasks or follow the list yourself.

5. **Use your dashboard and review it regularly.** The dashboard that I've shared with you is a suggestion, but be realistic. Do what works for you and review it.

Everyone is different, so you may have other items that I didn't mention in the top five that are more important to you. These are items that you know you have to work on above all else. You may want to make minor tweaks, or maybe you need to seriously transform and reinvent your business, but either way, you need to write it down. If you're reinventing your business or even just starting out and trying to ramp up your number of new clients, this is a great way to start every year. Consider using different product lines or services as a way to both reinvent and attract new, better, premium-fee clients.

CHAPTER 11

Getting It All Done—How to Create the 25-Hour Day to Implement Your Changes

At this point, you may like what you are reading (and I hope you do!). However, you might also be asking yourself where in the world you can get the time to implement all these changes.

I can tell you from personal experience, it's not easy. The reality is, no matter which new idea you may want to implement in the management of your firm, you still have commitments to keep. You have deadlines to meet, payroll and overhead to cover, and lots of clients at lower fees to serve. Yet, if you want to drastically change the way you are pricing your services, you're going to need to make the time to do this important work.

Tyranny of the Urgent

If you're like most accountants, you are probably finding yourself wishing there were 25-hour days. Surely, this extra time would relieve the tremendous pressure under which we live. The "to-do" list just never seems to get done—there are always emails to read, voicemails to respond to, people who need us at the office, people who need us at home. There's barely enough time in the day to stop and evaluate what we've accomplished. We are in desperate need of relief.

When you stop long enough to think about it, the time shortage dilemma goes much deeper than simply lacking enough hours in the day. It is basically a problem of priorities. Unfortunately, the most mundane tasks and noisiest complaints often get the highest priority. In the meantime, the things we'd like to do get shoved to the bottom of the pile.

There's also a mental payoff to working under this level of pressure. Think about the last time you worked at full speed for hours, completely engulfed in an important task. The end result of complete exhaustion is often accompanied by a sense of achievement and joy. Generally, it is the most urgent of requirements that produce this type of payoff, and so we live in a cycle. As we sense our failure to do what is really important, the oppression from the pile of unfinished tasks creates a sense of urgency.

So, we live in a constant tension between the urgent and the important. The problem is the most important work does not need to be done today; there is no immediate harm in postponing a week or even months at a time. Urgent though less important tasks call for immediate response with rising pressure.

A cycle forms in the tension between the urgent and important, and we feel regret and even shame from failing to do the important work needed to create a healthy business.

Unfortunately, this shame and feeling of failure may only intensify as you begin your own journey of pricing transformation. The easiest way to get the time you need to make these important changes is to create it!

Hunting for "Found" Time

So, where is the best place to look for more time? Some people say get into the office earlier, other people say stay later. Some of us have tried both. Some people suggest you come in and work on weekends and holidays, and all these can help, but they don't deal with the real, underlying time issue. So, what I like to tell our members here at CTC is that you don't need to work longer hours. You're likely already working too many hours as it is. Rather, you need to get more value from the hours that you're currently working. I love this concept because it not only makes it easier and possible to free up your time, it also focuses attention on the all-important aspect of value.

The first step in finding more time is to carefully audit the low-value junk time that you're already doing so that you can replace this low-value work with higher-order activities. I like to say: You don't have to do more and more in order to grow. You don't have to work harder, you just have to work better. You have to work smarter at those things that actually take up your time, and sometimes that is a process. In fact, all the time it's a process. It's a process to figure out what is the best use of your time. If there's not enough time to get it all done, then pick and choose your commitments that don't absolutely have to get done.

I like to refer to this as upgrading your use of time. And in order to upgrade your use of time, again, you've got to become fully aware of what takes up all your time currently.

It's really a myth that you don't have enough time. The fact is that you have all the time there is. Now, if you're sitting in an office right now by yourself, or you are at home or listening to this audio book in the car, I want you to say, right now, "I have all the time there is." It's so true. Don't you really have all the time there is?

The myth that somehow you can create more time is inaccurate. You can create more space for the things that deserve of your time, but you can't create more minutes or more hours in the day because we have all the time there is. I know this is kind of crazy, but the first time I really said this to myself many years ago, it seemed to really be confronting this myth or this illusion that I was carrying around at the time. As soon as I started saying out loud "I have all the time there is," suddenly it let me off the hook! I felt great relief in this idea because there is a way to control how you spend your time. Those who know me know that I am a control freak, and I really like things that I can take charge of. So, if that's true, and I do have all the time there is, and I can control how I spend it, then I can actually fix this issue of feeling like I don't have enough time.

But here's the thing: the commitments that take up our time during any given day are worth different levels of output or units of output. Isn't that true? I can spend time during my day folding the laundry, and I'm going to get a certain output from that input of time that I'm putting in. I'm going to fold the laundry, and my family is going to have fresh, clean clothes folded and waiting for them in their drawer, and personally, I find that payoff fantastic. I love finding clean laundry in my drawer, and I know that my family members enjoy finding clean laundry in their drawer as well. So, whatever input I'm putting in in terms of effort and time spent on things, there is an output; however, those outputs are of different value. Would you agree with that?

Here is another way of looking at the outputs of our time and efforts. If, on the other hand, instead of focusing my inputs on the laundry, I spend quality time with my family talking or playing a game, the results of that time spent provide a lifetime of memories. I may not always remember how many loads of laundry I've done in my life, but I'll always cherish the quality time spent with my loved ones. The results in this case are far more valuable to me.

In business, we can examine this same concept of inputs versus outputs based on the demands of our work. We can certainly spend hours reviewing email, sorting and organizing files, and searching for solutions to problems. But when it comes to certain business choices, the efforts of, say, making connections with sources of lucrative business clients or making key hires in the business can produce much better results. As such, the value of our efforts is much higher than the email and other administrative chores that we all succumb to.

The relative value of the output can also change over time. It's important to constantly audit your use of this valuable resource to make adjustments and gain better awareness of your actions if your goal is to upgrade your use of time.

In auditing your time, I like to evaluate what I'm doing using a letter grade. Similar to grade school, I refer to my activities at work as A, B, C, and D levels of time. An A is considered a high-value use of time, while a D is considered a low-value use of time. If you examine my two examples above, my time spent on the laundry would be a D-level use of time, while the quality time spent with my family I would consider an A-level use of time. In the business example above, the administrative work would be a D-level use of time, while the higher-value activities would be an A-level use of time.

You may be asking yourself about the necessity of D-level activities, and you would be correct in noticing that they are necessary. D-level activities are not simply those actions that are unnecessary; they are actions that generate a lower-value result.

However, necessary items that do not produce high-value results generally can be performed by someone or something else. For example, since my unique expertise is not needed to fold the laundry, I could have delegated that. Thus my time spent delegating would have been an even more powerful use of my time, and therefore the value of the output of that time is worth even more than the value of the output when I fold the laundry myself.

Is this making sense? I hope so, because when looking at our work on the technical side, sometimes it can be confusing. People can tend to be a bit delusional because we fool ourselves into thinking that maybe we are the only person who can do something in our office. This is especially true if you are a control freak like me! *Somehow I think so highly of myself, that I often perceive I am the only person on the planet who can do all the things I need to get done in my life!*

Once you're clear on how you're spending your time and which activities have greater value in outputs, it is time to delve deeper into the things that you do that create value.

As I've shared in earlier examples in this book, the common practice of bundling tax-planning services with a low-cost tax-return-preparation fee based on billable hours can certainly be profitable. After all, CPA firms for over a century have profited from their work. However, this same work can be much more valuable in a value-pricing scenario. Therefore, the output (the tax return and plan) is much more valuable when paid using a value-pricing model.

Applying Pareto to Pareto

You've likely heard of the Pareto principle. It is the economic theory that what we spend 80% of our time doing only produces 20% of our results. In reverse, the theory also states that 20% of your efforts produces 80% of your results. If you've ever tested this principle, it's an amazingly fun way to spend a weekend dissecting and testing the theory!

Taking this one step further: if we apply the same principle to the rule itself, it means 20% of those 20% of your efforts, produce 80% of the 80% of your results. This represents that just 4% of your effort generates 64% of your results!

In order to put this concept to work, however, you must be able to identify the "4%" activities that actually produce 64% of your results. Do you know what they are? When you understand this distinction and change your focus from "generating charge hours," to upgrading your use of time through the type of work you do in the hours that you work, the results are amazing!

As it is often difficult to really identify the high value activities in our work, here are a few examples of "4%" work: building systems that allow your team to function without you, creating processes to eliminate your Accounts Receivable, speaking at events where you can generate new high-value relationships for your firm, or the time you'll spend converting your business pricing model to premium pricing based on value.

When you master this skill, it's actually very easy to create the time you need to make important changes in your business. Working with thousands of CPA firms over the years, I often see firms doubling their bottom line within just 12 months of gaining clarity and upgrading their use of time. It's easy to see why. The results of the "4%" time are 64 times more valuable than the results you create now! For each hour of high-value time you reorganize for yourself, you can expect your results to grow by over 64 times!

The Pareto rule tells us that we economically spend the majority of our time on things that aren't going to produce the most compounded types of results that we're looking for. The goal I'd like you to consider is converting just five hours each week spent on D-level activities into A-level work. And here is the key: it's not just about getting rid of the D time. Unless you replace that time with A-level activities, which are 64 times more impactful, it really doesn't matter if you skip trying to do the D-level activities. It's what you do with those extra hours you gain that is the most important.

To find time, you need to focus on your D-level activities. When I say "focus," I mean focus on how to get rid of it. It still has to be done, and if you're the leader of your business, you are responsible for figuring out how it's going to get done, and, before that, even if it needs to get done.

Here is one way to evaluate these tasks efficiently. When examining each D-level activity, it helps to have a plan. I heard somewhere about a nifty system for getting rid of low-value work—it is described as "The 4 D's." The 4 D's are Delete it, Delegate it, Defer it, or Design it out.

Delete It!

The first strategy is to DELETE the task altogether. There are some low-level activities that just shouldn't be done by anyone. You've got to look at the action item and ask yourself, what are the consequences if no one does this at all? If the consequence of not doing the task is small, then just consider crossing it off your list altogether.

Delegate It!

Perhaps it's a task that needs to get done but not necessarily by you. If so, hand it off to your assistant, a staff member, a vendor, a partner. Any time you can hand off a lower-level activity to someone, you free up your time, and you can focus on doing more valuable work for your business.

Defer It!

Perhaps this task needs to be done and done by you, but should it happen right now? Sometimes, delaying the action is the smartest choice. I call that to defer; you could also think about as delay. There is a big difference between strategically delaying a task and procrastination. Earlier, I described the cycle of urgent and important work, and the tension generated from these demands on our time. Urgent though less important tasks call for immediate response with rising pressure. The simple act of creating space for your most important work can be accomplished merely by quieting the urgency of the less important work through deferral.

Design It Out

The last D stands for "design it out." When you find yourself or your team handling a recurring low-value activity over and over, instead of doing it, improve the process or system to keep the task from coming up in the first place! Design processes that can be automated either with a piece of technology or perhaps with systems that can help someone improve their efficiency with the task. This method simplifies processes. It also empowers your team, so that you can consistently get results with less and less reliance on you as the business owner.

Once you've mastered these steps to upgrading your use of time, you must constantly ask yourself, "Is this the best use of my time?" If not, use the 4 D's and free yourself up to create more value in your business. After all, if your price depends on value, you better be prepared to offer the highest value possible!

Conclusion

The problem today is that small-business accountants are working themselves to the bone because they can't charge enough in accounting and tax transactions to get the freedom that owning a small business is supposed to bring them.

The traditional tax industry is broken. I've made it my personal mission to identify—and locate the causes of—the most painful disadvantages of owning a tax practice, and I've created productive ways to change our businesses.

Being recognized for the value that we bring to client relationships not only improves our self-esteem and confidence but also changes the way tax professionals are viewed in general. The only way the public can realize the value that we bring them is if we tell them. I've found that the more I work to increase the value that I bring to my clients, the more I can charge for my expertise, and the fewer clients I need. Charging more allows me to build a quality team to support the business. The more I focus on proactively serving my clients, the more control I have over my business. The better service I provide, the more my business thrives. The more I focus on building my team, internal controls, and systems into my business, the less reliant the business is on me, and the more I can run my tax business as an investor rather than as an employee with a terrible boss.

As a business strategy expert for accountants and tax professionals, I've coached hundreds of tax business owners across the country and have identified three easy steps to increase your job satisfaction and give you the freedom you deserve.

First, gain a designation that shows off your expertise. Consider becoming certified in tax planning. The Certified Tax Coach designation denotes an expertise in tax strategy and proactive service. "CPA" and "EA" are valuable marks as well, but they just tell people what you are—not what you do that benefits them.

Next, get paid for your expertise by accepting fewer transaction-based engagements and more tax-planning and strategy-consulting agreements. These types of engagements are well suited for value pricing—a vehicle I and many other successful practitioners have used to create leverage in our businesses and serve our clients better by focusing on the value we bring.

Last, achieve freedom by systematizing your business and giving your team an "Extreme Staff Makeover."